Baring My Heart
CHANELLE HAYES

Baring My Heart
CHANELLE HAYES

By Chanelle Hayes
with Anna Pointer

JOHN BLAKE

Published by John Blake Publishing Ltd,
3 Bramber Court, 2 Bramber Road,
London W14 9PB, England

www.johnblakepublishing.co.uk

www.facebook.com/Johnblakepub ⨏
twitter.com/johnblakepub ⬛

This edition published in 2014

ISBN: 978 1 78219 982 3

British Library Cataloguing-in-Publication Data:

A catalogue record for this book is available from the British Library.

Design by www.envydesign.co.uk

Printed and bound in Great Britain by CPI Group (UK) Ltd

1 3 5 7 9 10 8 6 4 2

Papers used by John Blake Publishing are natural, recyclable products made from wood grown in sustainable forests. The manufacturing processes conform to the environmental regulations of the country of origin.

Every attempt has been made to contact the relevant copyright-holders, but some were unobtainable. We would be grateful if the appropriate people could contact us.

To my two mums: Without you, I wouldn't be who I am today. And to Blakely: Every day I grow more excited about who you're going to become.

Contents

Prologue

I will never forget the night of 30 May 2007, or the intense fear it imprinted on me forever after. As I was told to remove the eye mask and headphones I'd been wearing, I saw a blur of flashing lights through the car's tinted windows and a sea of people waving banners as music blared out around them. I felt sick to my stomach. There must have been hundreds of them – and they were all waiting for me: Chanelle Jade Hayes, a skinny 19-year-old student from Wakefield who, right now, was convinced she was about to make the biggest mistake of her life.

As an icy panic gripped me in the back seat of the car, I grabbed the driver's shoulder and screamed, 'Stop! I can't do this – I've changed my mind. I want to go home!' But he ignored me, apparently oblivious to my meltdown. Suddenly, the car came to a halt and I took a deep breath, saying to myself, 'Come on, Chanelle, you can do this.'

The moment I'd been waiting for was finally here – I was about to become a *Big Brother* housemate and spend the next few weeks living like a guinea pig, with my every move recorded by

TV cameras and played out to the entire nation. What the hell had I been thinking? Fighting back the urge to throw up, I really didn't think I could get out of the car, let alone go through with the show.

Still, there was no hiding place. This was live television and nobody in the seven-year history of *Big Brother* had ever bottled it on launch night. I couldn't be the first housemate to bail out, could I? As the car door opened, the paparazzi cameras flashed like crazy and I could hear the crowd booing and whistling. They had just watched my VT on the big screens, during which I had stripped down to my underwear, pouted and posed like my idol Victoria Beckham and basically acted like some pretentious idiot. No wonder they all hated me. But it was too late – I had to face their jeers.

Although my legs were like jelly and I was shaking all over, I just about managed to step out of the car without passing out. In the background, I could hear the presenter, Davina McCall, announcing random stuff like, 'Chanelle plays the violin to a Grade Seven standard and her favourite cheese is mozzarella.'

All of a sudden, the adrenaline kicked in. Wearing a Victoria Beckham-inspired grey dress – albeit from Miss Selfridge, rather than Prada – I put my little overnight case down and did a full, 360-degree turn for the bank of photographers jostling for position. I'd been practising my moves for the cameras for a while after watching various celebrities pose on the red carpet and had thought, 'Sod it, I'm going to have my moment!' But it really didn't go down well with the crowd. I guess they thought I was being arrogant and, to be fair, I definitely would have booed me too.

The walk up the stairs into the famous *BB* house was utterly terrifying; partly because I was wearing strappy black heels with big bows and I was convinced I'd trip over and end up splayed across the stage on my bum. But the worst thing of all was that I couldn't see anybody I knew in the crowd. I just wanted to see my mum or a familiar smiley face instead of all these hostile people taunting me like I was a pantomime villain. But there wasn't a single soul I recognised.

Desperate to get it over with, I paused by the entrance into the house, called out a feeble 'Bye!' and waved half-heartedly to the crowd. But it took all my willpower not to run back to the car and get the hell out of there. As the sliding doors painted with the famous *Big Brother* eye finally closed around me, the screams and catcalls vanished into silence. Thank God. I walked down the white-carpeted steps, took a few gulps of air and swore under my breath. Checking my hair in the mirror at the bottom of the stairs, I muttered to my reflection, 'What am I doing?' But there was no turning back. This was my new home, like it or not.

Opening the door into the living room, I nervously shrieked, 'Hi!' to the five other housemates who had arrived before me and, thankfully, they all ran over to hug me, which calmed me down a bit. Someone thrust a glass of champagne into my hands and I remember thinking how small the house seemed. It looks massive on TV but, in reality, it's like a little doll's house. Albeit one surrounded by dozens of cameras and prying eyes watching through one-way glass.

And so that was how I was first catapulted into the public eye seven years ago and, whether you loved me or loathed me that night, I think it's fair to say that I grabbed the public's attention from the very beginning. And while it was undoubtedly the most nerve-shredding moment of my life, I also instinctively knew that this was the biggest opportunity I would ever have to make my mark and carve a decent future for myself.

All this time later, I'm proud to say that is exactly what I went on to do. It hasn't always been easy but, of the 219 regular housemates in *Big Brother*'s British history, I've been one of the most successful and, thankfully, one that people still seem to like hearing about today.

So here, for the first time ever, is the full and candid truth about my rollercoaster life, in all its Technicolor glory. It's not exactly a comfy, fluffy read but I'm hoping it will enable you to get to know and understand the real me. And if all the hard times I've conquered offer even a tiny crumb of inspiration to anyone out there, opening up my heart in this way will have been more than worth it.

I hope you enjoy my story. Living it has certainly been one hell of a journey...

CHAPTER ONE

A Dramatic Start

S he knew immediately it was going to be bad news. Even in
the gloom of the early evening, my babysitter Sharon could
make out the grim expressions of the two policemen standing on
her doorstep.

Although I was only a tiny baby gurgling happily in my cot
when this all happened, I've played out the scene in my head
literally hundreds of times since I was first told about it years later.

Opening the front door, Sharon took a deep breath and said,
'What is it? Have you found her?'

'Miss Roberts, may we come in?' one of the policemen said.
'We need to speak with you urgently.'

'Oh my God, what's happened?' she said, following them into
the living room and closing the door behind her. 'Please don't
say she's...'

'You might like to sit down. We have some bad news, I'm afraid.'

'I don't need to sit down. Just tell me what's going on.'

'We are terribly sorry. But we do believe we have discovered
Ms Sinclair's body.'

'What, you mean she's....'

'It seems she has been murdered.'

'Oh Christ, no!' Sharon gasped. 'How... Where is she?'

'At the morgue,' said the officer. 'We know this is extremely distressing for you but we shall need you to accompany us there and formally identify the body.'

Sharon collapsed onto her knees and began to sob with a deep, despairing anguish. Or at least, that's how I've always imagined her to react – just like it was some horrific scene playing out on TV or in a film. But I can't be sure, seeing as I was only five months old at the time and blissfully oblivious to the nightmare unfolding around me.

As Sharon went off with one of the policemen, the other officer stayed behind to keep an eye on me. Down at the morgue, the dead woman laid out for identification was in a terrible state, with her body partially mutilated.

It was, indeed, the lady the police had assumed it to be.

Andrea Sinclair.

My mum.

Straight away, you can see that this book is not going to be your average celeb autobiography, glossing over the ups and downs of a young wannabe hell bent on fame and fortune. Although being famous has, of course, been an important aspect of my life thanks to my time in the *Big Brother* house in 2007, it is only a tiny part of the tale. The real story of my 26 years on the planet is far more dramatic and I hope after reading it you will understand a lot more about me: the tragedy I've had to come to terms with, the heart-breaking truths I've learned and the person I have become as a result of it all.

It's not easy to begin putting it all into words and I wouldn't have chosen my start in life in a million years. Especially as I made my entrance into the world behind bars. I was born on 11 November 1987 at HMP Styal, a women-only jail in Wilmslow, Cheshire. Well, technically, I didn't actually pop out of the womb in my mum's prison cell – she was rushed to Wythenshawe Hospital in south Manchester for the labour, before later being carted back to prison with me, a tiny, wrinkly babe in arms. Not exactly glamorous, huh?

By now, you may have sensed that Andrea had got herself into a real mess around the time she fell pregnant with me. And you'd be right there.

My mum was a prostitute. And while I was a growing little blob inside her belly, she was doing time at Styal for drug dealing. It was the typical kind of scenario: she'd left school with few qualifications, fallen in with the wrong crowd and then followed a slippery path into drugs and prostitution. Working the streets of Manchester and selling Class A stuff to slime bags, she was eventually busted. Although she'd dabbled with drugs herself – crack cocaine, heroin, ecstasy, coke, you name it – I've been told she was clean while she was expecting me, thanks to being locked up for the majority of her pregnancy. I guess that's something to be thankful for. Still, nobody ever had a clue who my real dad was – there isn't one named on my birth certificate.

This was all told to me a lot, lot later though. I never had the chance to hear it from my mum's own lips because I never knew her. Other than her cradling me in her arms while I was a tiny baby, we had very little time together.

By the time of that awful spring day, she had been released from prison and was trying desperately hard to turn things around. She was keeping off the drugs and doing everything in her power to carve out a brighter future for us – even looking for a tiny house in Huddersfield for us, along with my two older sisters, Melissa and Maria, who were both fathered by different dads to mine. But all of that hope was snuffed out in a millisecond on 5 April 1988.

As usual, when she had to go out, Mum had left me and Melissa with Sharon, saying she would be back the next morning. I like to think that she gave me a big kiss and cuddle before she left – although to think of it at all still hurts me like hell. But she can't have known what was about to happen, nor the fact that she would never see me again.

I'm not sure where she was going but she was apparently finding it hard to get work because of her criminal record. Anyway, it was completely out of character when she didn't come back the next morning as she had promised. In the end, it was my sister Melissa who first raised the alarm, saying, 'Sharon, there's something wrong with our mum. I just know there is.'

Around 24 hours after she had left, Sharon reported her missing to the police. There were no such things as mobile phones or email back then, so it was far easier just to vanish off the face of the earth. And it was the following day, by which time Sharon was tearing her hair out with worry, that the police turned up on her doorstep with their harrowing news.

After she had formally identified the body, things became a bit clearer. It turns out that one of her former clients had lured Mum to his grubby flat in Manchester. Goodness only knows why she went along with it but she did. And when she got there, this bloke, who was some nutter called Keith Pollard, strangled her to death with his tie. Once she was dead, he cut off one of her nipples and mutilated her body and then left her there in his flat.

What an utterly sick bastard. It sounds like a plot right out of *CSI* or something, doesn't it? I still can't even fathom how this happened to my own mum.

Why he killed her, and in such a violent way, has always been a bit of a mystery. They may have had a fight over money and there was one report at the time that said that she had tried to take some cash from his wallet. But nobody really knows – the details remain unbelievably sketchy.

So there I was, barely a few months old and suddenly without a mother. Or a father – well, not one that anybody knew about anyway.

After turning himself in, that vile beast Pollard was sentenced to life imprisonment in November 1988, aged 34. During his trial, he had pleaded self-defence, saying Mum had attacked him and that she had lunged at him with two knives in her hands. I may not have known her and, of course, I'm biased but I don't believe that for a minute. Everyone I've spoken to who knew her says she was a gentle soul, so I don't think she would have done anything like that unprovoked. And, thankfully, the court threw out his excuse that he was merely protecting himself. 'It is most unlikely that this was so and the jury did not accept the defence,' the court papers said at the time.

The judge in the case also drew on evidence from two psychiatrists, whose reports revealed that Pollard harboured 'perverse sexual interests'. Duh. You don't say! Pollard was also said to have been very depressed and subdued during the trial. My heart bleeds, even now.

As if this grim tale couldn't get any worse, I found out later that he had already been in prison before he attacked my mum, after savagely killing an elderly lady back in 1972. He broke into this poor old woman's home and stabbed her 70 times. Can you believe it?

Despite being sentenced to life in jail for that murder, he only served 11 years before being released. What a total bloody joke. The court papers show he was then sent back to prison for a couple of other more minor offences but was freed again in 1986 – just two years before he killed my mum.

The facts behind Pollard's case have plagued me ever since I first found out about all of this. Why does life not mean life? The simple but astonishingly painful fact is, if he had been kept in jail where he was supposed to be, my poor mum would still be alive today. Instead, she was betrayed by a woeful legal system that decided this man was fit to walk the streets. Even after all these years, it still really gets my blood boiling and, of course, makes me feel sad to the pit of my stomach.

While this was all chilling enough, I was once led to believe that Pollard was due for release from jail – a doubly scary threat, since I was well known by then. But as you'll see later, nobody within the prison services seemed to give a toss about the risk I may have been facing. It was like choosing to go on national TV in *Big Brother* made me fair game. Of course, there is always a price to pay for fame but I don't think being afraid for my own life was much of a deal at all.

Anyhow, let's go right back to the beginning. So much has happened to me since that terrible day when my mum had her life so cruelly snatched away but, at a time when I should have been showered in the love and comfort of devoted parents, I was completely alone in the world.

CHAPTER TWO

New Beginnings

After my mum's tragic death, I was temporarily taken into care, and my nan – Andrea's mum, Annie – did everything she could to adopt me. But Social Services decided she was probably too old by then and that I would be better off having a fresh start in life. For some reason, they wouldn't let my mum's brother Terry adopt me either. They just wanted me to have a clean break. All of this was so hard on Melissa and Maria, who were nine and fifteen at the time, because they had not only lost their own mum but now their baby sister had been taken away too. I know they found it absolutely devastating because they thought they would never even see me again. I've always felt so upset for them that they had to go through a double loss like that.

Soon after that, I was placed with foster parents – an amazing couple called Joan and Reg Singleton. They were an older pair, who lived in Golcar, West Yorkshire and never had children of their own. I was incredibly lucky really, as they were so lovely.

What's remarkable about them is that they fostered more than a hundred babies over the years. I remember a newspaper article when I was growing up about their commitment to taking in needy kids like myself; they literally had so much love to give. Joan especially adored little babies – and I'm told I was one of her 'special ones'. I guess the awful way in which my life had begun made her connect with me all the more.

Although I don't remember my days with them, she and Reg were the kindest souls. After I was adopted, I still went to see them every few months all through my childhood and I thought of them as my nan and granddad. Their house was so cosy and homely and full of special little hiding places. For instance, they had a musty old cellar, which I loved going down to as a treat. I'd fetch them bottles of dandelion and burdock – a strange fizzy drink made from plant extracts. They also had a greenhouse at the bottom of the garden and it was always my duty to go down there and check on the tomatoes, like it was this big adventure.

I also loved cuddling all the other babies they cared for in the years after I left. I remember thinking, 'That was my life once. I'm glad that other children now get to have some of their love too.'

The fact that I stayed in touch with Joan and Reg was rare because most foster parents never see a child again once he or she leaves, usually because the adopting parents choose to cut off all contact.

I'm glad to say it was a different story for my eventual adoptive parents, Harry and Christine Hayes, who I've known as Mum and Dad ever since they first took me home in the summer of 1988, when I was nine months old.

A hairdresser and a graphic designer, respectively, they met in the early 1970s and got married within a year, when Mum was 18 and Dad was 24. They both knew they wanted children early on but, for whatever reason, it didn't happen over the years, so they put their names down for adoption.

After a very long wait, where nothing happened at all, they decided to treat themselves to a luxurious holiday on the Amalfi Coast in Italy in early August 1988. And then, as if by fate, they got a call from their social worker – a lovely, kind lady called Christine Watson – the very day they returned home.

'We've got a little baby girl available for adoption right away,' they were told. 'She's called Chanelle and she needs a new home as soon as possible.'

Mum and Dad met with Christine that very same evening and, after hearing all about my plight, were determined to meet me and make me their own. Things began moving at lightning pace from that moment on and, eight days later, they came to see me with Christine at Joan and Reg's place. Apparently I had just started crawling at the time and was quietly fixated by the tassels hanging from the bottom of their sofa. Mum and Dad said they were smitten with me straight away!

With the initial stages of the adoption quickly approved, they had a lot to do over the following week – such as a trolley dash around Mothercare in Huddersfield, in which they bought everything in one swoop, including a cot, clothes, toys and all the other essential baby gear. They also took me to their little house in Earlsheaton, Dewsbury a couple of times to see if I settled in a strange new environment and, happily, I did – enjoying a contented afternoon nap in the new cot they had just bought me.

Then, on 31 August, they took me home for good. I had my own proper family at last. Speaking to Mum and Dad in later life about the whole process, I've realised that it must have been very difficult for them to adjust. While most couples have plenty of time to get used to the whole concept of parenthood, starting with pregnancy, planning a nursery and pre-natal classes, Mum and Dad had virtually no time to prepare and they certainly had no clue about babies. So thank God for lovely

Joan, who stepped in and showed them the ropes over those first few weeks. In fact, Dad remembers her teaching him to change a nappy, using a doll on the floor. It was all going perfectly well until he accidentally put the dress over the doll's face and Joan said, 'Well, the nappy is on OK but I'm afraid the baby died of suffocation five minutes ago!'

Although it was no doubt a crazy time for Mum and Dad, we all settled well into the new routine and I began walking at 11 months old. That November, I celebrated my first birthday, which was a special landmark for us all. My Uncle David bought me a cuddly toy called Wuzzle for the big occasion, which became one of my most loved teddies of all time. I also have Wuzzle to thank for helping me learn to speak because my very first word was 'Woowah' – a loose but distinct interpretation of his name! Another favourite companion was my toy rabbit, Betsy the Bunny, and I kept them both by my side for years. I even took Betsy into the *Big Brother* house with me 18 years later!

On 23 February 1989, the final adoption order was at last granted, much to Mum and Dad's relief. They still say that day in court was one of the most memorable of their lives, especially as the judge was such a nice man. After the legal proceedings had ended, this judge, a man called James Barry, presented me with a story book, as well as a card for Mum and Dad.

It said, 'Bon voyage. You have set out on a most important journey... May it be a long and happy one!'

They were so touched that they framed it and they still have it now. Later that day, they went to the pub with Christine, the social worker, for lunch to celebrate and then to a building society to open my very first savings account. Mum says she felt unbelievably proud and emotional to see the name 'Chanelle Hayes' written on the little banking book.

Unsurprisingly, I remember nothing of those days at all but

Mum and Dad managed to capture the early part of my life by making me a series of yearly diaries and a 'life book', with old photos and detailed descriptions of my progress.

In my very first diary of 1989, they wrote, 'To the little girl who has already given us more than we could ever have imagined. This book has been completed daily by Mummy and Daddy for a perfect little darling called Chanelle. We hope that she will treasure it always, as we will treasure completing it.'

Reading back over the diaries now, some of the entries make me laugh so much – like this one from 29 December that year, in which Mum wrote, 'Chanelle learned a new word today: "No." She repeated it over and over again. We put her to bed at 7.45 and she was still saying "No".'

Another day, they put, 'We went to Canthorne Park to feed the ducks but Chanelle thought it better to eat the bread herself than give it to the ducks.' That sounds quite typical of me!

To illustrate what a naughty madam I was, Mum wrote soon after, 'Today Chanelle generally got up to mischief. She was in and out of the fridge, playing with the toilet seat and throwing things in the loo. Later she had dinner – most of it ended up on the floor.'

All in all, I grew into a very normal toddler – albeit one that strongly knew her own mind from an early age. My favourite food was sausage with Yorkshire pudding and I was forever demanding that for tea – with the obligatory ketchup that I called 'sauce sauce'. And if I ever heard an ice-cream van chiming nearby, I'd drop everything and beg, 'Ice peam – want one!' And, of course, I almost always did get one.

Mum also tells me how she used to get me dressed in the mornings, only for me to get undressed again and throw all of my clothes down the stairs! She also once bought me a gorgeous, expensive dress with cute little bells on the bottom but I hated the tinkly noise and naughtily cut them all off when she wasn't looking!

I clearly liked fashion from an early age, as Mum says I was constantly rooting through her wardrobe, putting on her shoes and covering my arms in her bracelets and beads. One time, my diary records how Mum took me to see her twin sister – my Aunty Susan – who said to me, 'I like your top, Chanelle.' In reply, I looked her straight in the eye and said, 'It's a blouse.' Talk about headstrong – and I was only 18 months old at the time!

Without wanting to blow my own trumpet, it appears that I was developmentally well ahead of other babies my age, as a health visitor called Mrs Dickenson told Mum and Dad during a routine assessment around that time. 'It's remarkable,' she said. 'Chanelle is far more advanced for her age than any other baby I've seen in twenty years of doing this job.' What a result!

Mum and Dad say I was also very into singing and I woke them up most days belting out some nursery rhyme or other – even if I couldn't quite pronounce the words. One of the diary entries from back then says, 'I feel that maybe Chanelle might become a singer. She can even hit high notes, which are a little deafening at times. Even as I write she is doing a little solo act – and she doesn't like it if I join in.'

A few days later, Mum noted, 'Chanelle spent all morning singing away. Her voice is so strong and she is not a bit bothered about who hears her. Even the lady about six houses away has said how she good she is and that she thought it was the radio when she heard her. No, it was just Chanelle in the back garden.'

When I was two, Mum went back to work at her old hair salon and I would trot along with her most days. I think I actually became a bit of a star attraction for the customers, as I was always singing and dancing for them and would help put the hair nets on all the ladies' heads. Bless her, Mum still does hairdressing today but now she works at old-people's homes, doing all their blue rinses. And she still only charges them £3 a pop. I'll often say to her, 'Mum, how can you earn a proper living off that?'

And she'll say, 'Well, I'm thinking of increasing it by fifty pence soon.'

But she never does – she's so generous and kind-hearted like that.

One of my favourite things to do as a toddler was 'playing kitchens' and helping Mum make cakes. Well, I say I 'helped' but usually I was just licking cake mixture off the spoon. They've got an old photo of me practically with my foot in the bowl and Mum noted in my diary one day, 'Gave the mixing bowl to Chanelle and she put it on her head.'

Not quite *The Great British Bake Off*, was it?

Around this time, we moved house, to a bungalow in Middlestown, a small village outside Wakefield, where I started nursery school. Apparently I loved it and never once shed a tear when Mum left me there. I enjoyed learning, even at that age, and preferred activities that used my brain to playing with dolls. In fact, I only ever had one Barbie in my life and thought she was the dullest thing on earth!

My big passion was for stories and reading and, every single bedtime for years, my poor dad had to sit on the floor at the side of my bed, holding my hand and reading my books aloud. I wouldn't let him go and sometimes he'd be there for two hours before I drifted off to sleep and he could finally let go of my hand and creep out. He would often go straight to bed without any dinner afterwards because he was so exhausted. I adored Postman Pat and Beatrix Potter but my absolute favourite was Thomas the Tank Engine, and Dad – who often called me Jadey-pie because my middle name was Jade – says a typical exchange might go something like this:

'Night, night, sweetheart, it's time to go to sleep now.'

'No! I want to hear the one about Percy the Small Engine!'

'Come on, Jadey-pie, you've had lots of stories. You can hear all about Percy tomorrow.'

'No! Tell me it now!' And with a perfectly timed quiver of the bottom lip and a couple of stray crocodile tears, Dad always gave in. But in a way, I think we both look back on those times as a really important part of our bonding process. It was something that we did together; just the two of us, and I wouldn't change that for anything.

People have often asked me what it's like to have adoptive parents but I can honestly say that I don't think I feel any differently about them than if they were my own flesh and blood. I certainly grew up to love mine as if I had been born to them and, nowadays, it never really crosses my mind that I'm adopted. I know they feel the same way about me too. We've always been extremely close and, after everything we've been through as a family, that's what matters – not what's on my birth certificate.

CHAPTER THREE

Happy Days

In September 1992, when I was almost five, there was suddenly huge excitement in the air: I was going to have a new baby brother! Not due to Mum and Dad conceiving a child of their own but because they had decided to adopt again. Dad initially wanted to go for another girl but one day Mum sat him down and said, 'Harry, you already think you've got the best little girl in the world, so why give another daughter such a hurdle to leap over?'

'Hmmm. Fair point,' he said, thinking this through. 'Let's ask for a boy then.'

And that's how David came to be the fourth member of the Hayes family.

He arrived when he was around 15 months old and I was overjoyed that I had this new 'toy' to play with – although I caught chicken pox and then passed them straight on to him within a few days of him settling in!

David was endlessly fascinating to me but Mum and Dad insisted I was very gentle with him because he'd had a traumatic start in life too. David's birth mother had been abusive towards him and, as a result, he was quite behind in his development. He wasn't yet walking when he joined us, simply because he hadn't had enough time or attention spent on him. That all changed really quickly though and the social workers were amazed at how quickly he flourished in Mum and Dad's care.

But, while I was majorly excited by this new person, like most kids who are faced with a new sibling stealing all the limelight, there were times when I did find him pretty annoying. One time, I remember hitting him around the head with a pillow and saying to Mum, 'I've had enough of David. Can you make him go away now?'

His presence also made things more cramped in the house. We lived in a converted bungalow and the bedrooms upstairs were tiny. Mine was probably the smallest of all, with just a bed and chest of drawers for furniture. I used to have to walk on the bed just to move around – it was like Harry Potter's room under the stairs!

One thing was quickly clear about David and me though: we were like chalk and cheese. While I was loud and confident, he wouldn't say boo to a goose. But we grew close over time and have always considered ourselves brother and sister. In later years, we both went to the same schools and, though I was four years above him, I became very protective of him. Because he was one of the quiet ones, people pushed him around a lot, which I'd get so angry about.

One time, his little friend came up to me when I was on prefect duty and said, 'Are you David Hayes' sister?'

'Yeah. Why?' I said.

'Well, this lad keeps stealing his lunch money and he's just letting him get away with it. I thought you'd want to know.'

That got my blood absolutely boiling. 'Right, who is it? What class is he in?'

I went to this boy's classroom and dragged him out, saying I needed to speak to him about a prefect matter. When I got him outside the class, I pinned him up against the wall.

'Listen here, you little shit,' I said. 'If you ever take my brother's dinner money again, I'll kill you. Do you understand?'

Looking absolutely terrified, he just nodded and then wrestled free and ran off down the corridor. After that, he never did it again! I never told David but he must have known I'd stepped in, as the bullying stopped from that day onwards.

David was never particularly academic but not everyone has to be the Brain of Britain, do they? Nowadays, he's 22 and works in the local branch of Sainsbury's, which he's more than happy with. He's a hard-worker and that's all that matters.

At home, David and I always knew we were adopted – it wasn't some big secret that Mum and Dad kept from us. The life book they made for me explained that I used to have a different mummy but that she had gone away 'to Heaven'. Mum and Dad never went into any detail about it – why would they? I was too young to know about anything horrible like that. The book also explained to me that I had two half-sisters, Maria and Melissa, but again, being so young, I never hankered after more information or asked to meet them. It was just the kind of information you soak up as a kid – a bit like knowing that you never cross the road without holding your mum's hand. If I did ever ask any questions about my past, my parents would simply say, 'That was your life then, this is your life now.' It was only much, much later that this answer was not enough to satisfy my curiosity.

When I started 'big school', at Middlestown Junior, I took to it like a duck to water and pretty quickly established myself as 'top of the class' in all subjects. I was a total swot and teacher's pet, and Mum and Dad say nobody ever uttered a bad word about me in my school reports or at parents' evenings. It was all, 'Chanelle doesn't even have to try at her subjects. She breezes through everything.'

Singing continued to be a speciality of mine – and I went through a phase of making up lyrics, including an oddly profound number about God, in which I sang, 'Don't let people die.' On a cheerier note, my absolute favourites were the songs from *Calamity Jane* and *Chitty Chitty Bang Bang*, along with Rod, Jane and Freddy – my parents once took me to see them live in Barnsley, much to my excitement. You could say I was a bit of an exhibitionist really – if there was music playing in a shopping centre or wherever, I'd just start singing and dancing, showing off like some hyperactive performing monkey!

So you can imagine how much I loved going to my weekly ballet lessons. The opportunity to dress up in a leotard and tutu and prance around for an appreciative audience was a dream come true for a girl who loved stealing the limelight. I also wore my Brownie uniform with pride and took real pleasure in getting my various badges – for all those things like making tea and being kind to animals. Somehow those accomplishments seemed so very important at that age. My partner in crime at Brownies was my close friend Alison, who I grew up with, and we thought it was extra amazing because her mum was Brown Owl, so we'd parade around every week like we were top dog!

When I started at my secondary school, Horbury High, I continued to be a bit of a clever-clogs and got really into studying foreign languages. I loved Spanish and decided in my early teens that I wanted to become fluent and move to Spain. For a long time, my dream job was to be a speech therapist in the sunshine.

The only subjects I wasn't so keen on were History and Geography – although now I wish I'd paid more attention because these days I get really worried about natural disasters like tsunamis. Can you get a tsunami in Yorkshire? I'm not sure but I still panic about it!

Alongside all the academic stuff, I'd usually bag a lead role in whatever plays or concerts were going on at school. I once played Juliet in a version of *Romeo and Juliet* and, to this day, Dad says I was so good that I could have cut it as a professional actress. I'm still waiting for my call from Hollywood, obviously.

As for sports, I think I still hold Horbury's record for the high jump! But, while I enjoyed athletics and running, I hated hockey because I got so bruised and I found trampolining boring and stupid too.

My biggest talent of all though was playing the violin and I got up to Grade Seven, which was quite a personal achievement. I joined Wakefield Youth Orchestra and loved the buzz of playing in big concerts at the city cathedral. Sometimes I still get my old violin out now and have a little go – but I'm a bit rusty these days.

I think one of the only times I got badly into trouble was when I was supposed to have a TB immunisation and I refused and ran out of school. I've always been so terrified of needles (even now, if I have my lips done or a bit of Botox, I can't stand them)! The next day, my teachers had a massive go at me and threatened to take my prefect badge off me. But after I'd grovelled a bit, they changed their mind.

Family holidays were always a highlight of growing up and, though we never went anywhere fancy or abroad, we used to have the best time at Center Parcs. We used to go to the one in Nottingham every February and it was brilliant because my friend Alison would come along and we could just run wild for a week. It's so safe there and Mum and Dad never had to worry about what we were getting up to (or so they thought). We'd spend most of our time in the pool and on the slides and checking out boys, of course! I still have very happy memories of those days.

In the summer holidays, we'd usually go and stay in a caravan at Bridlington. It wasn't exactly the Costa del Sol but I usually took Alison along and we always had fun. Mum and Dad would give us each £10 every morning and we'd make it last all day and into the evening. It's amazing how much we managed to stretch our precious funds: swimming in the morning, a bag of chips at lunchtime and a trip to the arcades in the afternoon. Then at night, we used to cake ourselves with make-up and go to the on-site club to watch rubbishy bands. We felt so grown up!

We still sometimes go back to Bridlington as a family now but last year David said, 'I'm twenty-two, for God's sake. I don't want to go to a caravan and spend a week in the pouring rain.' Fair enough, I guess.

While my school days were pretty ordinary, the summer of 1996 sparked a change in me that would go on to shape my life for years to come. It started when I was 10 years old, after I heard a really catchy song playing on the radio. Putting two and two together, I realised this was the new pop group that everyone was talking about: the Spice Girls. Has there ever been a more memorable debut than their first single, 'Wannabe'? I seriously doubt it. One listen for me and a major addiction was born.

Like millions of other youngsters, I loved the song's ballsy lyrics – all that stuff about the guy needing to be accepted by the girl's friends. I'd never heard anything like it before and loved the band's feisty image and their 'Girl Power' message. I soon became obsessed with them and would save all my pocket money to buy merchandise. I had a Polaroid camera, posters, towels, duvet sets and a Spice Girls body spray – which actually smelt like cat wee, though I still wore it, of course! I had all the cassettes and video tapes and then, when their stuff came out on

CD and DVD, I had to get those too. At least knowing what to buy me for birthdays and Christmas was an absolute doddle!

The great thing about the group was that they were all such different characters, so you could pick who you wanted to be. Everyone had a Spice Girl they could relate to and, for me, it was initially Geri Halliwell. I even coloured my hair red with one of those wash-in, wash-out dyes – which looked disgusting! Then I began wearing a bra and stuffing socks in it because Geri had big boobs and I had absolutely nothing up top at that age. I liked the fact that Geri was so gobby too. You got the impression she wouldn't stand for any nonsense.

Still, in the fickle way that you do as a kid, I soon grew a bit bored of Geri in all her flamboyant Union Jack gear and, as quickly as I had latched on to her, dropped her for Posh Spice. She had recently started dating David Beckham and, like the whole nation, I was intrigued by this glamorous pop-star/footballer combo. Their romance seemed like such a fairy tale and I devoured all the glossy-magazine shoots and interviews they did around the time Brand Beckham took off. It seems naff now but all the matching clothes, David in a sarong and the 'his 'n' hers' thrones at 'Beckingham Palace' were so fun – even if they wouldn't be seen dead doing that kind of thing today.

As you'll discover throughout this book, Posh has maintained a very steady presence in my life since then – even if she might not realise it! I've always loved watching her style evolve and the fact that all of her looks tell a different story. When the Spice Girls first strutted onto the scene, she would typically wear leopard-print fur coats, teeny leather bras and mini-skirts but that changed drastically as her fame began to soar. I used to pore over pictures of her ever-changing hairstyles and increasingly expensive outfits and shoes, and craved the lifestyle that she and David had.

Then, when the golden couple had their first son, Brooklyn, in 1999 and got married that same year, my adulation took on a whole new dimension. I loved the fact that, while they both worked hard and looked so good, they were totally family orientated – something I admired even when I was young. Apart from for a couple of years in my life when I hit the party scene, I've always been a stay-at-home girl at heart. I think, because of being adopted myself, the idea of the family unit has always been crucially important to me. I looked up to Victoria for not only being stylish and gorgeous but also having such strong maternal instincts. She and David were the perfect role models in my eyes.

All in all, my childhood was very happy and I was lucky to be surrounded by a close-knit family. I was especially fond of my Aunty Jean – who was married to Dad's brother Basil. One vivid memory I have of her is that she was the first person to ever get me drunk! It happened at some kind of family party when I was about 13 and she kept passing me Bacardi Breezers under the table. By the end of the evening, I was pretty tipsy and hiding the fact I couldn't quite walk straight from Mum and Dad was a real challenge! Aunty Jean only died recently, which was so sad, but I'll always have fond memories of our naughty collaboration that evening.

As well as Aunty Jean, I adored Joan and Reg and the only real sadness I knew in those days was when they both died during my early teens. He passed away first and then she followed not too long after. It was almost like she couldn't bear to go on without him. They were very much that kind of couple and I still think of them often.

CHAPTER FOUR

A Need for Answers

Although I never thought much about my real mum and what happened to her when I was a little girl, something suddenly changed in me by the time I reached 14. I had this nagging feeling that there was a lot of important stuff I should know about – a sixth sense maybe.

I remember speaking to our old social worker Christine about it. We'd always stayed in touch over the years and I said to her, 'How did my real mum die? Do you know?'

She hesitated but said gently, 'Look, I can't tell you that. It's not up to me to make that decision. That's up to your mum and dad, so you'll have to ask them.'

Naturally, that only increased my curiosity further and something in her tone convinced me there was something awful I should know about.

I didn't want to make too much of a big deal of it because I didn't want to upset Mum and Dad by poking around into my past but, when I put them on the spot and asked how my real mum had died, they both became very cagey. Of course, if you

23

refuse to answer a teenager's questions, they will automatically want to know at least a hundred times more urgently. So, though it had never been an issue before, it was now something I thought about a lot and was determined to get to the bottom of.

Over the coming months, I started asking my parents about her constantly but they felt I wasn't ready to handle the truth. I've always been a stubborn little thing though and the brick wall they put up just made me more hell bent on finding out the truth. While my mates were more concerned with chatting up boys or scraping together funds for the latest shoes in Topshop, I was busy playing Miss Marple to piece together the clues I had about my mum's life.

Because I was so preoccupied by whatever had happened, I started having recurring nightmares. I'd dream I was being kidnapped and then wake up, sitting bolt upright with my hair all sweaty and stuck to my face. It was always the same scenario – I'd be shopping in town and there would be this weird-looking guy in black clothes. His hands would come out of nowhere and snatch me away from a woman, who I guess was my real mum.

'Let go of me!' I'd yell but the man would just grin at me and then, as the woman disappeared from my sight, I'd wake up. I got so scared that I even refused to go into town with Mum for a while.

What was rapidly becoming an obsession started to make me difficult to live with. It felt like there was a big conspiracy to keep these missing strands of my history from me.

'Mum, will you please just talk to me and respect my wishes?' I'd ask her. 'I really can cope with whatever the big secret is, you know.'

'Oh, Chanelle,' she would say. 'I know you think you're old enough but, when we adopted you, we made the decision not to tell you until you were older and we have to stick to that. It really is for your own good.'

When I got tired of that kind of conversation, I'd try a more direct approach and corner her as she was making breakfast or putting on a load of washing.

'Tell me now,' I'd demand, without even wishing her a good morning. 'I have a right to know how she died. You owe it to me.'

'Chanelle, we've talked about this so many times and, when the time is right, your dad and I will tell you everything. But not yet.'

These words were so infuriating. 'So when will the time be right?' I'd snap. 'What's the difference between now and in two or three years? You're so mean to keep this from me. I'm not a kid anymore!'

But it was hopeless; Mum wasn't going to budge. And whenever I brought up the subject with Dad, I'd get a firmer response still.

'When you're eighteen, you'll be an adult and you can find out everything you want to know. But not now. That's the end of the matter.'

Why couldn't they see that I needed to uncover my past, just to know who I really was? The more they blocked me, the angrier I got. Fights became an almost daily occurrence and I remember once storming up to my room and slamming the door so hard the walls shook.

'I hate you both!' I screamed, throwing myself onto the bed and burying my face in the pillows. 'Nobody understands what I'm going through. It's so unfair!'

I must have sounded like a stuck record – and God knows how my poor brother put up with all the commotion. But then David was always a calm, placid boy. He would sit quietly in his room on his PlayStation while, all around him, World War Three was breaking out and then casually emerge half an hour later, saying, 'What's for tea, Mum?' It must stem from his own past because his real mum used to beat him black and blue if he so much as made a noise.

While I was going through what could probably be described as a bratty phase, I decided to get a tattoo. And not just a tiny, subtle initial on my wrist or something but a full-on, massive design right across my lower back. I had to use fake ID to get it done, which I'm not proud of, but now I hate the thing. It's vile and, if it didn't leave a white mark behind, I'd have it removed in a flash. It makes me feel physically sick and I insist on having it airbrushed out of my modelling pictures. Overall, I'm not a fan of tattoos on girls – and while we're on that subject, Cheryl Cole's bottom is the most repulsive thing I've seen in my life. What on earth was going through her mind?

When I got mine, it was quite funny though because, for about five years, I let my dad believe it was a henna tattoo and that I was having it topped up regularly. Only when I went on *Big Brother* did he realise that it was real and he yelled at Mum, 'This is disgraceful! Why didn't you tell me she had this monstrosity?'

Poor Mum said, 'I'm sorry, Harry but she told me not to say anything!'

Getting a hideous tattoo and fighting with Mum and Dad non-stop illustrates how frustrated I was becoming at home and I felt that I couldn't really share my problems with anyone. David and I were close but we didn't share those kinds of things and I think I wanted to protect him from it anyway. And, of course, my friends didn't understand what I was going through. None of them were adopted, for a start, and they certainly hadn't had mums who'd died in weird, unspoken circumstances.

As I could never share what was eating away at me with my mates, they were a bit baffled as to why my home life constantly resembled a battleground. We'd meet up and they'd be like, 'What's up with you today then?'

'What do you think?' I'd say. 'I've had another fight with Mum and Dad – I bloody hate them.'

'Oh, just the usual then.'

Well, not exactly. What we were dealing with here were not typical teenage strops about pocket money or staying out past 11pm. That stuff seemed so trivial to me. This was a much bigger issue and, if I'm honest, I really didn't know how to handle it. As my rows with Mum escalated, she'd simply refuse to talk to me or send me to my room.

One day, when I had turned 15, after arguing for about the zillionth time, Mum told me cryptically, 'There are things you don't understand. And you won't be able to understand them until you're an adult.'

'But I am grown up enough now,' I protested. 'Everyone says I'm very mature for my age. I've even got two jobs.'

I was working part-time as a waitress at a nearby hotel called Cedar Court and thought this surely proved how responsible I was.

'Chanelle, please just let it go,' she said with a sigh. 'My decision is final. You are too young and that's that.'

Then, as a tide of frustration and anger washed over me, I yelled, 'What do you know? You're not even my real mum!' As my temper boiled over, I couldn't stop. 'I don't know who you think you are but you can't tell me what to do! You have no right!'

It must be like a slap in the face for any parent to hear such vicious words and I could tell in an instant how badly I'd wounded her.

'You are not my real mum!' I repeated, out of sheer desperation. Seeing the pain fill her eyes as my words sank in, she looked like a broken woman.

Looking back, I wonder how I could have been so cruel. It makes me feel sick that I intentionally tried to hurt her like that. Mum would do anything in the world for me and my brother, so the way I treated her still haunts me. Thankfully, she has forgiven me for all of that now but sometimes I look back and can hear myself shouting those nasty words. It's then that I want to call her just to tell her how much I love her.

CHAPTER FIVE

Rebellion

With my relationship with my parents deteriorating, I decided that, if they were going to treat me like a baby, I might as well behave like one. So that was when I decided to run away. With all my questions and tantrums getting me absolutely nowhere, it seemed like a good way to make a stand to my parents and punish them at the same time.

One night, after a big fight, I was pacing my room, feeling so angry and like I had nowhere to turn. 'I have to get out of this house,' I said to myself. The situation was quite literally driving me crazy.

It was dark outside and, when I was sure that Mum, Dad and David were all downstairs watching TV, I shoved a change of clothes and some schoolbooks into a carrier bag and climbed out of my bedroom window. Dropping onto the garage roof, I then jumped into the bushes beneath. This was a pretty big deal for me, as the idea of being a tomboy appalled me and I'd have much preferred to use the front door. Incidentally, those bushes were a mess for ages afterwards and my dad moaned for an eternity about the Chanelle-shaped dent I left in them!

Wanting to cause as much worry as possible, I didn't bother to leave a note before I left but instead scrawled some horrible comments in the life book they'd made me when I was little. There was a really cute baby photo of me with them, which they'd captioned 'Chanelle with her new family'. Cruelly, I wrote underneath, 'Well, you're not much of a family, are you?' I wish I hadn't done that now. It was such a lovely book and I'm still upset I spoiled it like that.

At the time, I didn't care about hurting them. I just wanted to be out of the house, so I'd scrabbled together a few pounds in cash and caught a bus to Wakefield train station. I was trying to look as grown up as I could but, in reality, was absolutely petrified. I almost didn't go through with it and contemplated getting the bus straight back home again. But I had a point to prove and that determination somehow pushed me on.

Even though it was fairly late in the evening and a good hour and a half away, I'd decided to go to Hull, where a girl I knew called Emma lived. She was a bit older than me but Alison and I had met her on holiday a few times and had a right laugh with her. The train pulled in to the platform and I got on, praying I wouldn't see anyone I knew and that I wouldn't get stopped for a ticket. As I didn't have much money, I hid in the toilets for the entire journey. The stench was totally revolting and churned my stomach but I kept saying over and over to myself, 'Just a little bit longer. They'll be so worried by now. Serves them right.'

When I arrived in Hull at around 11pm, I called Emma from a pay phone. If she hadn't been in, I had absolutely no back-up plan in mind. But I would probably have slept rough at the station, rather than go home. Fortunately, she picked up the phone after a couple of rings.

'Hi, it's Chanelle,' I said sheepishly. 'I know you're not expecting me but I've come to visit.'

'Are you kidding? You're mad!' she said, laughing and not knowing the half of it. 'It's late – why didn't you tell me you were coming?'

'Um, it was a spur of the moment thing. I wanted to surprise you.'

'Well, you've done that. OK, wait there and I'll come and collect you.'

Emma picked me up on her scooter and, as soon as she saw me, she said, 'Let me guess. You've fallen out with your folks.'

'Yep. Majorly,' I said and nodded. 'I hate them.'

She smiled sympathetically. 'Right, tell me all about it later. Hop on.'

I put the helmet on and climbed on behind her and we set off for her mum's place a few miles away. But within minutes, just after we joined the M62, we were faced with a total disaster.

'Shit! The police!' Emma said, as a flash of blue lights appeared behind us.

'Shit!' I echoed, as she pulled over onto the hard shoulder. 'What will we say? I'm not going home. Please don't tell them I've run away!'

With both of us panicking, the policeman approached us and said, 'Do you know it's illegal to ride a scooter on the motorway?'

'Er, no. I'm really sorry,' Emma fibbed. 'I had no idea. But I won't do it again, I promise.'

'Well, I still have to impose a penalty fine. You've broken the law and you were posing a serious danger to yourself and other motorists.'

She gave her details to the officer, as I sat there praying that would be the end of it and we could scoot off to her mum's house via some country lane instead. But the look of terror on my face must have been a giveaway because the policeman then asked for my name and address. After I'd told him, with my heart thudding, he frowned at me.

'So what are you doing here this late at night? Wakefield is a long way away. Do your parents know you're here?'

'Yes. Well, kind of. Anyway, they won't mind. They know Emma,' I stammered.

'How old are you please, miss?'

'Er, I'm fifteen.'

The policeman sighed and looked at his watch. It was at least 11.30pm by now and he looked as if he really could do without the hassle so late in the evening.

'I think you had better come with me to the station,' he said. 'We can call your parents and ask them if they're happy about you being away from home.'

'No, please. It's really OK. They're fine with me doing what I want. You don't need to call them,' I begged. 'Please just let me go home with Emma.'

But he was adamant and insisted we both go to the police station, which was so humiliating. My first attempt at running away and I couldn't even make it through a couple of hours before being found out.

'Mr Hayes, I'm sorry to disturb you at this hour but I have your daughter Chanelle here at Hull police station,' he said into the phone. There was a pause. 'Yes, she's safe and well. But I take it you didn't know she was here?'

There was a pause. 'No, I thought not.'

As their conversation continued, I sat with my head bowed, feeling like such a baby. And though I tried not to cry, I couldn't help it.

Emma hugged me. 'Don't get upset,' she said. 'You can come and visit me another time.'

'It's not that. I'm just going to be in so much trouble,' I said.

'Don't worry, it'll be fine,' she tried to reassure me. 'They'll just be glad to get you home.'

'You don't know my dad,' I said, sniffing.

Then I heard the officer say, 'Yes, of course. We'll look after her here until then. See you later.'

It turns out that Mum and Dad hadn't realised I'd gone until they got that call – no doubt assuming I was tucked up in bed and fast asleep.

In desperation, I tried one more time to win over the officer. 'Do I really have to go home? I want to stay here with Emma.'

It was no use. 'Yes, you do have to go home, young lady. You've got two very concerned parents back in Wakefield. Do you realise the risk you put yourself in by not telling them where you'd gone?'

I said nothing and stared at the ground. And as I waited for Dad to pick me up from the freezing cold police station, I felt nauseous about his reaction. When he arrived an hour or so later, he looked pale and worn out but he didn't even need to say anything. I could tell from his expression how angry and disappointed in me he was.

We drove back without speaking a word. Mum was still up when we got home and she dashed to the front door and flung her arms around me when we arrived. But then she took a step backwards and the expression on her face changed drastically.

'What on earth were you playing at? You can't just go off on your own without telling us. Anything could have happened and we would never have known where you were.'

Feeling too exhausted for a big scene, I ran straight upstairs to my room and shut the door. I climbed into bed fully clothed and remember crying myself to sleep.

Next morning, I feared the worst but, weirdly, it was like nothing had happened. I think Mum and Dad must have decided that creating more drama would not get us anywhere. I was prepared for a full-scale row but, instead, they seemed to want to bury it and carry on as normally as possible.

But within weeks of that, the tension soon built up again and I decided to go to Bridlington, where we often used to go on our caravan holidays. There was a girl called Jo, who Alison and I had become friendly with the summer before, so like a homeless stray, I turned up on the doorstep with my things and begged to stay. My plan was just as ill-thought out as before though, as her mum insisted on calling my parents and I was carted back home again, embarrassed and furious in equal measure.

But just like last time, Mum and Dad were happy to brush over what I'd done.

'I hope we can draw a line under this behaviour now,' Dad said. 'You need to live by our rules if you want to stay in this house, OK? We can't have you skipping school either. Your education is too important.'

I could see that this much was true. And, while I was mortified to have made such a mess of running away again, part of me was relieved to get back to school. I genuinely didn't like missing my lessons so, after that, I vowed to stop the disappearing acts.

CHAPTER SIX

First Love

Things with Mum and Dad went from bad to worse. They still refused to talk to me about my real mum and lashing out at them was the only way I could express myself. I remember, during one enormous row, I tore into them, shouting, 'Why did you ever bother adopting me? You obviously don't love me!'

The tension in the house wasn't helped when I started seeing this boy from school, called Scott, who was a couple of years older than me. Dad instantly disliked him, as he'd heard on the grapevine that he was a bit of a bad boy, into drugs and hardcore partying.

'What do you see in him?' he asked me. 'He's no good. Trust me, a father knows these things.'

Nothing is more effective at making you keen on a guy than your dad's disapproval, so I paid no attention at all. I presumed Dad was just upset because he had correctly guessed that Scott and I were sleeping together. Despite me only being 15, I always felt really mature for my age, so sex just seemed like a natural progression.

Scott and I had known each other as kids, when he lived next door to Zoe, one of my best friends. Her parents have always been close to mine, so she's more like family to me than a mate. She's one of the nicest people I've ever known.

Anyway, the three of us would hang out together and play football against the wall by his house but his family moved away and I forgot all about him. A few years later, they came back to the area and he turned up at our school again. Zoe grabbed me in the playground one lunch time and, giggling, said 'Bloody hell! Look who it is!'

She was pointing to this good-looking lad having a kick-about with the boys and said, 'It's him! You know, the guy who used to live next door to me.'

'Oh my God!' I shrieked. 'He's fit now!' And he was. Scott was tall and dark and looked really cool, in that 'doesn't give a shit' way. Eventually, I plucked up the courage to talk to him.

'Oh, yeah, I remember you,' he said, looking me up and down approvingly. 'Well, you've grown up, haven't you?'

We got on well immediately and it wasn't long until he asked me out, much to my excitement. Scott just seemed so worldly wise and, even in his school uniform, he looked way older than me. Despite only being 15, I felt at least 21 in my head and I wanted nothing more than to be a fully-fledged adult.

As a result, losing my virginity to him a month or so later didn't seem like a big deal at all. Sure, it was a bit awkward when we first slept together but when isn't it? I still hate having new partners, even now. Scott had been asking over and over when I'd be ready to 'do it' but he seemed OK to wait. The day it finally happened, his parents had gone out and we went up to his bedroom for the inevitable. He put a Tracy Chapman CD on, which sounds unbelievably corny now but, at the time, it felt so sophisticated. Cheesy or what?

Although he seemed to know exactly what he was doing, being that bit older, I'm afraid to say that it wasn't some mind-blowing experience for me. In fact, it was pretty forgettable and I was left thinking, 'Is that really it?' How overrated it was. 'Where are the dramatic noises they make in films?' I thought. 'Why is my mind not being blown right now? And why am I thinking about the essay I've got to hand in tomorrow?'

Still, I was glad we'd done it, mainly because I now thought I was so damn grown up. We were nearly caught out though, as his parents came back soon after and said, 'What's going on here?' I'm sure we looked pretty sheepish as we emerged from his bedroom protesting our innocence but they probably had us well sussed.

After that, we began sleeping together regularly – whenever we could really. I was already on the pill, as I'd had some cysts on my ovaries, so we didn't have to worry about contraception. And I guess I thought I was in love. Looking back now, that relationship barely even registers on my radar now but it was so important back then. It felt so liberating, especially as I felt like I was being treated like such a baby at home.

The fact that my parents didn't like him and wouldn't let him sleep over at our place meant I began spending more and more time at his house. One time, Mum turned up there looking for me, clearly worried out of her mind, but I stayed up in his bedroom, trying not to utter a sound.

'Is Chanelle here?' I heard her ask at the front door. She sounded fraught with worry but I didn't move a muscle. 'I'm worried about her. She hasn't been home for three days.'

'No, she's not here Christine,' Scott lied through his teeth. 'I haven't seen her. Sorry.'

I felt bad for deceiving her but it was easier to do that and a small part of me enjoyed making them worry. But, when I did show up at home again, Dad was livid.

'Get out of this house!' he blasted. 'If you refuse to respect your mother and me and how we run this house, you might as well leave for good.'

So off I stomped back to Scott's place, my hiding place from reality. The only trouble was it wasn't long after this that Scott unveiled his true colours. And it turned out that my dad had been right to be wary of him: he was a total druggie. I discovered that he was doing a lot of ecstasy with his mates and, despite me at first thinking it was entirely up to him if he wanted to pump his body full of dangerous chemicals, it began to affect our relationship. The drugs made him act so selfishly – like the time I cooked him a special Valentine's meal at his house. I'd slaved over a hot oven and got us a nice bottle of wine but, in the end, he turned up really late that evening, without letting me know where he was. I ate the meal on my own, feeling utterly sorry for myself. When Scott finally showed up, he couldn't eat anything because he was gurning so badly. I was so upset. But I also couldn't go home because I knew I wasn't welcome there. I had no choice but to forgive him.

At this stage, I of course had no idea about my real mum's drug problems, or even who she was, so it's odd how I've always been quite anti-them. It's almost like I had some sixth sense from birth about what had happened to her.

Scott never quite understood my attitude either.

'Just try one pill – you'll enjoy it,' he'd say.

'No thanks,' I'd scoff. 'There's no point. I hate drugs. It's such a dirty thing to do.'

It's a view I still hold very strongly today but, back in my fiery teen world, I was about to put my parents through one of the most horrendous tests of their lives.

CHAPTER SEVEN

A Cry for Help

I had settled into this kind of horrible, destructive pattern with my parents, where I was basically living with Scott but would occasionally turn up at home to pick up some clothes or books – and fly headfirst into another row. One day, we were fighting about my 'lack of respect' towards them when I simply felt that I couldn't take any more. As the sparks flew, I could feel my anger rising like a big ball of fire.

'How can you have a go at me about this trivial crap when you're hiding such big secrets from me?' I yelled. 'You know how much it means to me to find out the truth about my mum but you won't just do that one small thing for me. That's the reason I'm always at Scott's – because I can't stand being here with you! All you do is lie to me and treat me like a stupid idiot. I won't put up with it any more, OK?'

As they stared at me, stony-faced, I shrieked, 'You don't care about me. Not one bit. Why are you keeping this from me? If you were good parents, you'd just tell me. I've had enough!'

Mum tried in vain to calm me down. 'Look, we're not going

into this all over again,' she said. 'Now dry your eyes and just try and see it from our point of view for once.'

They both left the room and I suddenly felt like I didn't belong with this family at all. 'These people don't even love me,' I thought. 'The only person who loved me was my real mum and she's dead.'

I wasn't in control of it but something inside me had snapped. I'd tried reasoning with them, I'd tried shouting and screaming, I'd even tried running away and I felt there was nothing else I could do. I just couldn't cope with it any more.

I'd never had any suicidal thoughts before but, all of a sudden, my next move seemed blindingly obvious. Looking back, I feel mortified that I could have hit such a low point at such a young age but what I did next seemed to make perfect sense. It wasn't something I had planned at all but I knew exactly what to do. I went into the lounge and took a bottle of whisky from my dad's drinks cabinet and stormed up to the bathroom with it. I could hardly focus because I was crying so hard but I locked the door and got on with it. I'd seen this sort of thing on TV shows like *Casualty* and it looked easy enough. There were a load of painkillers in the bathroom cabinet, which I knew would do the trick.

I caught sight of my face in the mirror and it shocked me. My eyes were wild and mascara was streaming down my face. I remember thinking how much older I looked, like there was a huge weight on my shoulders that should never have been there.

From the noise I'd made and the sound of my crying, Mum and Dad realised I was up to something and started banging on the bathroom door.

'What are you doing, Chanelle? Let us in!'

'No! I've had enough.' I screamed. 'You don't love me! Go away!'

There was no stopping me now. I was completely hysterical.

'I don't want to live here any more. Let me leave or I'm going to swallow all these tablets!'

Mum again begged me to open the door. 'We can sort this out, just don't do anything silly,' she shouted.

Dad, too, was beginning to sound panicked. 'It doesn't need to be like this. You're our daughter. We love you.'

'I don't care what you say,' I screamed. I don't think that I really wanted to die but, the way I was feeling, if there had been a button I could have pressed that would just turn everything off, I would have hit it in a flash.

I started rifling through the half-used packets of paracetamol, aspirin and ibuprofen and began popping the pills out of their foil packets and forcing them one by one into my mouth. Somehow, I knocked them back with slugs of whisky, which tasted absolutely vile and smelled just as bad. Even a faint whiff of the stuff these days makes me feel queasy and I haven't been able to swallow tablets properly since then either.

I have no idea how many pills I took but it must have been about 20. With the hammering on the door becoming more and more frantic and the booze and tablets starting to take hold, I decided to go one step further. I went to the bathroom cabinet and reached for my dad's razor.

I sat on the edge of the bath and began stroking the blade across my left wrist. I watched in some kind of semi-conscious trance as the blood sprung from my veins and ran over my arm in thin streaks, covering my fingers and dripping onto the floor. God, it stung so badly. It was absolute agony. The cuts weren't very deep but I've never known pain like that and I still have the small scars on my wrist today.

You might be wondering if I secretly liked the pain I was inflicting on myself but, in all honesty, I absolutely hated it. This was not about self-harm for me, where you cut yourself to let stuff out and make yourself feel better. I wasn't doing it for relief, I just didn't know how else to make myself heard.

It must have been about then that I passed out – from a combination of the blood loss and the effects of the pills and whisky, I guess. Fortunately, my parents had already called an ambulance and, as it raced towards our house, Dad managed to force open the bathroom door with a knife.

'No! Chanelle! What have you done?' he screamed as they barged into the room and found me lying almost lifeless on the floor. They wrapped my wrist with a towel to stem the bleeding and, thank God, the ambulance arrived moments later. I was rushed to Wakefield General Hospital and taken straight through to have my stomach pumped. Obviously, I was out cold through all of this, so the only recollection I have after blacking out is of waking up in my hospital bed, feeling thoroughly dazed and sick. When I did come round, I remember looking down at my bandaged arm, wondering, 'What the hell was I thinking?'

As the reality hit home, one of the doctors told me, 'You're a very lucky girl. If you'd taken many more tablets, you wouldn't have had the choice of living or dying. Your organs would have been so messed up that you wouldn't have stood a chance.'

I couldn't believe I had come that close to dying, and just wanted to get out of the hospital. The doctors and nurses kept coming over to put tubes in my arms, or write a list of confusing figures on their clipboards, and I'd continually ask, 'Can I go home now?'

'Not yet,' they told me, again and again. 'The effects of the tablets can take a while to show up and sometimes they can cause long-term damage to your insides – even days after the overdose.'

This was the last thing I wanted to hear and a small part of me actually wished I had died. At least then there would have been a point to it. But, as it was, I felt like I'd failed and that people would think I had only done it as a pathetic cry for attention. That was mortifying when all around me on the ward there were really poorly children suffering from cancer and terminal illness they had no control over. I kept thinking, 'You selfish cow, Chanelle. At least you have your health, unlike these poor little things.'

When Mum and Dad came to see me, I just burst into tears as they approached my bed.

'Hello, Jadey-pie,' Dad said and smiled. 'How's my girl doing?'

Mum sat and held my hands and I couldn't understand why they weren't furious with me.

'I'm OK,' I said with a shrug, wiping away tears. 'Aren't you mad at me?'

They shook their heads and said, 'We just want you to be well. Nothing else matters.'

'So you don't hate me for doing this?'

'Of course not,' said Mum. But, like before, they really didn't want to dwell on my behaviour. 'Look, we just want you home,' she said. 'We don't need to talk about why you did it. We can just put it behind us and move on.'

When I did eventually go home, I knew how badly I'd upset them, so I agreed to start seeing a new social worker to address my 'issues'. She was called Becky and I'll be frank – she was a total idiot. I was going through the worst time of my life and yet she'd turn up saying, 'Right, today we're going to draw some pictures to identify our feelings.'

I was like, 'Becky, let me be honest with you. I know I'm only fifteen but I'm not stupid – I don't need the Crayolas. I'll speak to you on a level but don't even bother with this.'

In reality, I've always found it hard to tell people how I really feel. My stomach would go into such knots whenever anyone asked me anything remotely heavy, so perhaps Becky never even stood a chance of getting through to me. But still, she drove me absolutely mad in her attempts.

'How are you feeling today?' she'd ask. 'Why don't you draw how you feel?'

So I'd say sarcastically, 'Well, I can either draw a sad face or a smiley face. That's about the extent of my talent in arts and crafts.'

I know it sounds ungrateful when she was only trying to help me, but this was not how to give therapy to a troubled teenager like me. One time she said, 'If you draw me a picture with these felt-tip pens, next week we can try it with paints.'

Jesus Christ, what was she thinking? 'What? I'm fifteen years old,' I snapped. 'Are you joking?' Fair enough, that kind of psychobabble might have worked on four- or five-year-olds but it was just insulting to me. 'Becky,' I said, 'I'm not trying to be rude but this is ridiculous. If you want to talk to me, that's fine. But don't expect me to sit here drawing stick men and smiley faces.'

And she replied, 'Well, what about if we make a chart about how you're feeling? Has it been a sad day, a good day or a medium day?'

'I'm not drawing a chart either,' I said. 'I'm not three and I'm not wetting the bed. This is just not working for me.'

Those sessions with Becky used to make me so angry and I'd inevitably take it out on Mum.

'Why are you making me see that woman? I'm not some imbecile,' I'd say.

In the end, Mum arranged for my previous social worker Christine to step in – and she was a breath of fresh air because I trusted her implicitly. She picked me up from school sometimes and took me to Pizza Hut, so it felt like a treat, rather than some kind of psychobabble session. We could actually talk about stuff, without her forcing me to draw daft pictures. I used to enjoy our chats because she never seemed to judge me or have any expectations of me. And if I felt angry and bitter towards my mum and dad on any occasion, that was fine too. She always encouraged me to express my emotions and that helped me a lot.

But while she was a calming influence in my life, the next almighty storm was already brewing.

CHAPTER EIGHT

The Truth At Last

Although things settled down a bit in the months after my suicide attempt, my impatience to know the truth never left me and, pretty soon, it was gnawing away at me more than ever. One day, I was in the car with Mum when I got stuck into her again.

'Look, I'm getting older now,' I said, 'so I really do think you can tell me about my mum.'

She refused to discuss it and wouldn't even look at me. I must have been having a bad day because I then screamed at her, 'You're just an evil bitch!' This was bad because, in all our fights, I'd never sworn at her before. But what she said in reply really took my breath away.

'Well, do you know what, Chanelle? Carry on like this and you're going to be no better than your mum.'

'What did you just say?' I fired back. 'What the hell do you mean by that?'

But Mum realised she'd let slip more than she wanted to and would say no more. 'Nothing. I meant nothing. Just drop it. This is definitely not the right time.'

I couldn't make her tell me anything else and we fell out badly over it once again. Things got so bad that I decided to move in permanently with Scott and his family. His mum, Lynne, was brilliant right from the word go.

'Stay as long as you want,' she told me warmly. 'I know you're having a tough time, so you're more than welcome here.'

It was nice of her but Scott was still into his drugs and it became quite a regular occurrence that I'd cook for him and then end up throwing his food in the bin while he 'tripped out' at the table.

All the signs were there that Scott was going to hurt me badly, so perhaps it shouldn't have surprised me when he announced casually that he'd got another girl pregnant.

'What?' I froze when he told me, my jaw literally hanging open. 'How could you do that to me? I trusted you!'

I ran into the lounge in floods of tears and broke the news to Lynne, who was disgusted with her son.

'I want you out of this house, Scott,' she told him coldly. 'Chanelle would never cheat on you in a million years – how dare you treat her like that?'

He didn't have much to say to that and got his stuff together that same evening. He moved into a caravan and my world was in bits. He had been everything to me and him cheating on me was like having my one and only emotional prop kicked out from under me.

Full of despair, it was in their house that I took my second overdose. Just like the last time, I decided I wanted to flick the switch off and end all of my pain. Grabbing a bottle of gin from Lynne's cupboard, I went up to the bathroom and started swigging it with some painkillers. Almost methodically, I then found a razor and scored a couple of small cuts on my left wrist. Little beads of blood shot out, just like before. It was so easy but, in the blink of an eye, I changed my mind and thought, 'What the fuck am I doing? This is stupid. I need help.'

Clutching my arm, I staggered downstairs and wailed, 'Lynne, I'm so sorry! Look what I've done! I've taken all these tablets too. Please help me. I'm in a really bad place.'

As ever, she was so calm and knew exactly what to do. She called an ambulance and then phoned Scott, who joined us at the hospital. Fortunately, the cuts were no way near as bad this time and I hadn't taken enough pills to pose any serious risk to myself. I was allowed out that same night and, as I didn't want to talk to Scott or even look at his cheating face, Lynne took me back with her. As good as she was in the crisis, she said later, 'I feel like it's all my fault.'

'Don't be silly,' I said. 'Of course it's not.'

After that, I decided to go back home because there was no point in me staying with them after Scott left. But old habits die hard and pretty soon, I'm ashamed to admit, I started phoning him again. Unbelievably, I begged him to take me back.

'I don't care if you got that girl pregnant,' I grovelled. 'I'm so unhappy without you, please can we try again?'

I can't believe I was such a fool now but we did end up getting back together and, with his encouragement, I started bunking off school. He had quit by then and didn't want me going in without him, mostly because he was worried about other boys flirting with me. Scott was always a complete control freak – he used to work in a bowling alley and he liked my friend Natalie and I to get the bus there every Saturday and hang around all day. I'd met Natalie in Year Seven at high school and we were as thick as thieves. Even now, we're still very close. But when we went along to the bowling alley each weekend, we didn't even play – we just sat there chatting because Scott liked to keep an eye on me. I loved him though and I'd have done anything to keep hold of him. How pathetic does that make me sound?

At this point, I was about to sit my mock-GCSE exams and

my teachers were concerned about the number of lessons I was bunking off. They had repeatedly called my parents to tell them and this was what Mum and I were fighting about on this particular night.

'You can't keep skipping school, Chanelle. You need to get your education or you'll never make anything of yourself,' she said.

I sat in silence, refusing to even look at her.

'What are we going to do with you? Your dad and I are at our wits end.'

'Stop telling me what to do!' I spat back. 'You're always criticising me. It's no wonder I hate living here!'

As the fight went round in a circle for what seemed like the millionth time, I screamed, 'Right! I've had enough. I'm going into the woods and I don't want you to follow me.'

'Why are you going to do that? It's pitch-black out there,' she reasoned.

And I thought, 'Because if I stay in this house, I'll bloody well go into the bathroom and take some more pills.'

So I stormed out to the wooded area behind our house, which was also a shortcut to Natalie's house. Because it was dark, I called her on my mobile and she ran to meet me and we walked to her house together. I was crying so hard I could hardly walk straight. When we got there, her mum Anthea gave me a big hug and sat me down.

'What on earth is the matter?' she asked. 'What could be so terrible?' I could barely speak for the tears but then, without even meaning for it to happen, it all came pouring out. I told them about everything I'd been through and why I couldn't take any more. It was an enormous release of pressure.

When I'd finished recounting my traumatic few months, Anthea looked a little dumbstruck but stood up and said, 'OK,

Chanelle. I think this has gone on long enough. I'm going to call your mum.'

And as I sat there sobbing, she dialled our home number and I heard her say in a hushed voice, 'Christine, I'm sorry to interfere and I know you have Chanelle's best interests at heart. But I don't think things can go on like this. Something's got to give here. It's bad for her, it's bad for you and I think you need to be honest with her. This is destroying her. I'm worried that, if it goes on, she might really be pushed over the edge and it'll be too late then.'

Finally, someone was actually talking sense. I'll always be grateful to Anthea for that because what she said really got through to Mum at long last. She came over straight away, still in her dressing gown, and has since told me that the next hour was among the hardest of her life.

As soon she walked into the kitchen, I wiped my nose and said, 'Are you going to tell me then?'

She looked like a rabbit caught in the headlights and Anthea said, 'Girls, go and wait in the living room. I need to talk to your mum now, Chanelle.'

At least someone was there to take control of the situation. It seemed that neither Mum nor I was capable of that.

Natalie dragged me by the hand into the living room and sat me down on the sofa but I was in such a state that I kept trying to get up and go back into the kitchen.

'Sit down,' Natalie urged. 'Let my mum talk to her first – she knows what she's doing.'

It felt like they were in there for an eternity and, though I was straining my ears to catch what was going on, I could barely hear anything over the thudding of my heartbeat. Every now and again I heard a little bits of a muffled conversation and, at one stage, I'm sure I heard Anthea gasp out loud.

Finally, the door to the living room opened.

I jumped up. 'What is it? Tell me.' I stared directly at Mum.

She glanced at Anthea, shaking her head. 'I can't do this,' she whispered, holding her head in her hands.

'What?' I shouted. 'Stop these games! You have to tell me now. This isn't fair.'

'Come on, Christine, you know you have to do this,' Anthea said softly, putting her hand gently on her shoulder.

As Mum sat down, she sighed deeply and I noticed that tears were rolling silently down her face. In all our fights over the years, I had never seen Mum cry and something registered in the pit of my stomach what a big deal this must be.

'OK, Chanelle, I have wanted to protect you from this all your life but, if I really must tell you, I will.' She took a deep breath. 'You think your mum died because of an accident or illness and we've always let you believe that. But that's not the case.' She paused and composed herself again. 'She didn't die of cancer, or in a car crash, or because of anything else like that.'

Another deep breath. 'Chanelle, your mum was a prostitute. She was murdered.'

I felt a rushing sound in my ears. I must have misheard.

'What?' I said slowly, my voice barely audible. 'No way,' I whispered, shaking my head. 'You're lying. It can't be true.'

'I'm not lying, it's the truth. I swear,' she said. 'Why would I make this up? Your mum was strangled to death by one of her clients when you were five months old. You were sent to foster parents and then we adopted you soon after. We didn't want to tell you until you were older. We've always felt it would be too much for you.'

Mum had come and sat next to me on the sofa but I wasn't able to listen to any more. Of all the scenarios I'd imagined over the years about my real mum, it had never even crossed my mind that she might have been killed. I was completely lost for words.

'I don't believe it,' I must have said 20 times. 'How can this be happening?'

Nobody knew what to do or say after the big announcement and, after a few minutes, Mum got up.

'Here's £10 for your dinner money for the rest of the week if you want to stay here but you're more than welcome to come back with me. It is still your home, Chanelle, and we love you very much.'

But I couldn't move. I couldn't do anything. I couldn't even look at her. So she went home and I sat shaking in the chair, feeling like I might pass out. Anthea handed me a big glass of red wine.

'This will help calm your nerves,' she said.

I hated red wine in those days but I gulped it down quickly and can't remember much about the rest of the evening. But, bizarrely, I do recall that, when we finally went to bed, with Natalie and me lying top to tail in her bed, I started thinking about my Spanish oral exam the next day.

The phrases I'd been practising were going round and round in my head for some reason and, in particular, the topic about my family. You know the kind of thing you have to learn verbatim; those sentences like, 'In my family, I've got a mum and dad and one brother.' It suddenly seemed so ironic. Imagine if I'd said, 'I've got a mum, dad and brother – oh, and another mum who was a hooker and got murdered by some sicko bastard.'

I don't think I slept the entire night. My mind was racing and I kept hearing Mum say those chilling words: 'Your mum was a prostitute... she was murdered.'

The next day, I felt like death but forced myself into school for the exam. God knows how but it went well. I barely spoke to anyone all day and I brushed off my friends' concerns every time they asked me what was wrong. I needed some time to get my own head round it before I could tell anyone else.

Natalie and Anthea helped me through the next couple of days by giving me space when I needed it and a shoulder to cry on as the news began to sink in. I couldn't begin to make any sense of it but, after a few days, I knew I wanted to go home and start repairing my relationship with Mum and Dad. I knew that I had to salvage the family I still had, while I still could.

CHAPTER NINE

Revisiting the Past

Although our relationship was still on shaky ground, things were much better at home when I moved back in. I had a new respect for Mum and Dad for telling me the truth and knew instinctively that I didn't want to fight them any more. Although it was the most horrific piece of news to come to terms with, I felt calmer inside. For me, knowing what had happened – no matter how distressing – was a lot easier to cope with than being kept in the dark. It had also made me realise how badly I'd treated them both.

'I'm sorry I was so awful to you,' I told them. 'But now I know, it won't happen again.'

They smiled sadly and both held me for a long time.

Naturally, I had further questions about the murder and it seemed that Sharon, my babysitter, had only been able to identify my mum's body by a birthmark on her leg. Who knows the full extent of what the psychotic killer, this loner called Keith Pollard, did to her? I'd actually prefer not to know.

The only shred of comfort I can take from the tale is that

Mum's body wasn't left lying there for too long. Pollard handed himself into the police after killing her, which was why they found her so quickly in his flat. She was later cremated in Sheffield – though, of course, as a baby, I wasn't there for that. My two sisters Maria and Melissa did go, which I know they found totally devastating. I never knew her, of course, but they were the ones with all those memories to lose.

Although Pollard has served his time after being jailed in 1988, the probation officers say it's highly unlikely now that he'll ever be released. We were told that he did appeal a few years ago but that his behaviour has not been good enough and he hasn't shown any remorse. It's strange knowing so little – we've never even known what prison he was sent to and just assumed it was one of the high-security ones in Manchester. I do thank my lucky stars that he's still locked up though. Ultimately, they have to think of public safety and the fact that he also murdered that poor old lady. In my opinion, he's best off where he is.

I know we're meant to believe in rehabilitation and all of that but it's too hard to forgive and forget when it's your own flesh and blood that's been snatched from you. I will never simply shrug my shoulders and wish him well, or say that he might be a reformed character, because that would be disrespectful to my mother's memory. I hate him and I always will do.

After I came out of *Big Brother*, there were reports that he was set to be released, so I went to see the prison officers and told them my own safety could be at risk if he was back on the streets. What a disaster.

'He'll know exactly where to find me if he's freed,' I told this stern woman in a starchy white blouse. 'I have been on TV recently, so he might know who I am.'

You'd think my concerns were valid but this horribly unsympathetic lady just replied, 'Well, you chose to put yourself in the public eye by doing your job. That's not something we can help you with.'

I couldn't believe what I was hearing. 'You mean, because I've chosen to make something of my life, I am going to be punished for that? I could be an anonymous cleaner and that'd be OK but, because I am famous, it would be my fault if he knew where to find me?'

I was absolutely incensed but the woman showed no understanding for my situation at all. She said, 'You could get a restraining order, meaning he won't be able to approach you, but we can't have him watched or tracked because that would be against his human rights.'

'What?' I shrieked. 'His human rights! What about my rights? Or the rights of my dead mother? He should be in prison forever after what he's done, never mind his bloody rights!'

I was so outraged. It seemed like a complete and utter farce and I couldn't help thinking that things would have been very different if Pollard had killed two little children, instead of a prostitute and a pensioner.

As I struggled with my disbelief, I asked the woman if Pollard was ever allowed to read newspapers from his cell. I had been doing a lot of modelling and was suddenly horrified that he might have seen some of my pictures.

'I can't say,' she said. 'That would also be an infringement of his rights. But I can confirm that he would be able to buy any newspaper should he so wish.'

For Christ's sake, this was just outrageous! Why did my rights matter so little when I was the innocent person here? He was able to know stuff about me if he wanted but he was protected by this web of bureaucracy. Where's the justice in that?

'Does he have pictures of me on his walls?' I asked, feeling queasy. But this fell on equally deaf ears. 'I can't tell you that either,' she answered. 'But he is free to put pictures and photos on his wall, yes.'

I gave up at that point – I was getting nowhere. But, to me, this was all so very wrong. Not to mention bloody scary.

Rewinding back to my 15-year-old self, once I'd moved back home, there was another bombshell for me to deal with. Mum came into my bedroom and said, 'Can we talk?'

'Sure,' I said, sitting up on my bed. 'What is it?'

'Well, now you know the truth about your real mum, it's probably the right time to give this to you.'

She sat on the bed and handed me an envelope.

'It's a letter from Annie, your nan. Your mum's mum. She wrote it when you were given up for adoption and we've been saving it for you, along with some other things she and your sisters Maria and Melissa have sent you over the years.'

Then she handed me a bag containing a whole load of presents, birthday cards and photos from them, which she and Dad had been storing up for all this time. God knows how they kept them all secret from me – I thought nothing went unnoticed by me. I was gobsmacked but comforted to know that they hadn't forgotten me in all those years. Opening the envelope, I smiled at Mum and said, 'Thanks. This means a lot.'

The letter from my nan was written the day after I was given up for adoption and it still reduces me to a sobbing mess every time I read it now.

It said:

My dear Chanelle, I am very sad just now, as yesterday I saw you for the last time and had to say goodbye.

By now you will be grown up and I just know that you will be beautiful. I hope and trust that you have been happy and content with your new parents, and they with you, and always will, as they chose you especially.

Your real mum will be watching over you because she loved you very much, just as she loved your sisters Maria and Melissa.

Tears were rolling down my face. It was the saddest thing I'd ever read. The letter continued:

I am your nan (your mum's mum). At the time of writing, Maria is 15 and Melissa is 9 years old. How old they will be when you read this will be up to your adopted parents. I am sure they will choose the right time for you.

We were all devastated at the time of your mum's death, the circumstances of which you will no doubt by now have been told. It was very tragic and your mum didn't deserve such a terrible death.

If by any chance you are wondering why none of the family kept you, it just wasn't feasible. I wanted to but I was too old to give you a proper life and, of course, your sisters were too young. So we thought the best thing possible for you was to let you go to your adopted mum and dad and pray that you would have a loving and caring relationship.

I hope and pray that we did the right thing. I am leaving some photographs with this letter in the hope that it will give you some idea of your mum, your sisters and me.

Your mum didn't always do the right thing but, whatever she did, she loved all of us and did what she thought was helping us. She had a heart of gold and would help anyone and we miss her terribly.

As you can imagine, this was almost too much for me to bear. I'd obviously never known of the impact Mum's death had on those who knew and loved her, so it was heart-breaking to read of their pain and loss.

She ended the letter:

> Well, love, I know I probably won't be around when you are of age but I am hoping and praying that you will try and contact Maria and Melissa and, through them, find the rest of the family but it is entirely your decision.
>
> It has been a rather difficult letter to write but I have done my best. Assuring you once more of our love for you, I will close this letter. I will always be thinking of you and wondering how you are. Goodbye, love, and please try to contact your sisters.
>
> All my love for always, from Nan xxx

Phew. What a colossal thing to take in. I felt moved beyond words and sat utterly speechless on my bed.

'Are you OK?' Mum asked.

I nodded. 'It's just so beautiful. I don't know what to think.'

'We knew it would upset you. That's why we had to wait until you were older. It's a hell of a lot for you to take in.'

I took a deep breath and started to look through the photos she'd enclosed with the letter. The first thing I noticed was how much I looked like my real mum. It really was spooky, as if I was seeing old black-and-white pictures of myself from another lifetime. There was one shot of her cradling me as a baby – I can only have been about a month old when it was taken – and it's one of my most treasured possessions. I keep it next to my bed even now.

Next, I turned to the letter my two sisters had sent.
Maria wrote:

> Chanelle, I will love you always.
> I just hope you will try to find me when you want.
> I want you to keep the photos and locket always (even
> if you don't want to find your proper family). I will
> understand if you don't want to get to know me,
> Melissa and your nan because I know how hard it is.
> Lots and lots of love always, Maria xxxx

And Melissa had written, 'Chanelle, yes, I am your sister. I just
want you to know I love you very much. Please do not forget me
because I love you a lot. Your own sister, Melissa x'

It was short and sweet but equally touching – especially from
a nine-year-old.

The letters threw me into turmoil because I knew I had to get
in touch. I'd never thought about seeing them before because I
was so young and they just weren't on my radar. It's like being
told you've got a distant second cousin out there somewhere.
You might think, 'Oh, right. That's nice,' but you don't drop
everything and try and find them. Also, I guess, subconsciously, it
would have seemed disrespectful to Mum and Dad to open that
can of worms.

But now the invitation was on the table, it was different. I
needed to know if my nan was still alive, for starters. She
sounded like such a lovely lady from her letter.

After I had read and re-read all the letters a few times, Mum
said, 'Christine at Social Services was wondering, would you like
to meet them all?'

'Um, I think I would,' I said and nodded. 'If you and Dad
don't mind.'

She shook her head. 'No, we'd never deny you that chance. You have our full support, whatever you want to do.'

So I discussed it with Christine and told her that I was keen but also terrified.

'What are you frightened of?' she asked.

'I've never been part of their family, so they might hate me,' I admitted. 'A lot of time has passed since they wrote those letters.'

She smiled. 'I'm sure they won't hate you. The link you have is so strong, it might bring you together.'

But she also warned me that meeting them could open up a lot of new wounds. 'As much as you have in common, it may still be very difficult and painful for you all. So much time has passed and you know nothing about each other, so it won't be plain sailing. This is a decision you have to weigh up very carefully.'

I thought hard about what Christine said but I knew instinctively it was something I had to do, so I told her to go ahead and contact them. She got back to me almost straight away and said, 'Right, I've approached your sisters and your nan and all three want to see you.'

'Wow. OK,' I said. This was really going to happen.

We agreed that to see all three of them at once might be a little overwhelming, so Christine arranged a meeting with Nan first for a week on Saturday. When that day came, I was so nervous I nearly called it off. But Christine picked me up and said, 'Come on. You can do this. If you hate it, you never need go again.'

When we pulled up outside her house in Sheffield, she led me to the door and rang the bell. After a couple of minutes, this little old lady opened the door and just stared at me agog, as if she'd seen a ghost. After a couple of seconds, her face lit up.

'So you must be Chanelle!'

She reached out for me and gave me a hug. I felt like a plank of wood and, when she finally let me go, she was crying. She was really frail and seemed quite weak.

'I've dreamed of meeting you for years and years,' she whispered, clutching my hand and holding it firmly. 'You look exactly like your mother. It's just unbelievable.'

She studied my face again. 'I had no idea you would be the spitting image of Andrea. I'm so shocked.'

As she led us into the lounge, I noticed old black-and-white photos of my mum, in which she did look astoundingly like me.

Over a cup of milky tea, Nan and I took the first tentative steps towards getting to know each other. It was so nice to meet her but I couldn't get my head round the fact that the elderly woman before me was my own flesh and blood. This was my nan – someone I should have visited every weekend during my childhood and drawn pictures and bought endless bottles of sherry for. But I had been denied all of that. Could we even begin making up for that now?

We talked for an hour or so and she was genuinely so sweet – asking about my studies at school, what my hobbies were and that kind of stuff. When it came time to leave, she took my hand again.

'Please come and see me again soon, Chanelle. I'm not getting any younger and we've a lot of lost time to make up for.'

'Yes, I'll come back soon,' I promised. In retrospect, I only wish I could have realised the significance of her words then and how little time we actually had.

As Christine drove me home, she asked me what I'd made of Nan. I thought for a while.

'It was really hard.'

'Why? Didn't you like her?'

'No, it's not that,' I stammered. 'She's adorable. It's just, well, I just don't know how I'm meant to react.'

Seeing Nan cry upon meeting me had left me feeling so confused – should I have cried too?

A couple of days later, my mixed feelings made a little more sense to me. 'I know what's really bothering me,' I told Christine. 'Nan loved my mum to pieces but I can't share that love because it's for someone I've never known.'

'Go on,' Christine urged. 'Keep talking.'

'I just feel a bit cheated really. I'm gutted that I didn't get to spend any time with my mum, and both my sisters and my Nan did. It's not fair, is it?'

'I think you've hit the nail on the head,' Christine said, nodding. 'But you mustn't feel guilty about it. Don't be too hard on yourself.'

Two weeks later, she accompanied me to Maria's house so I could meet my sisters. Nan was there too and, when we arrived, Maria and Melissa ran to the door and both burst into tears as soon as they saw me.

'Oh my God, she is just like our mum!' Maria choked.

'I told you, didn't I?' said Nan, reaching out for me.

'It's unbelievable,' Melissa added, staring at me intensely.

I swallowed hard and said politely, 'Hi. It's very nice to meet you both.'

As Nan ushered us into the lounge, I realised we were not alone. There was a baby sleeping in one corner of the room and another little boy playing with his toys on the floor.

'Meet your nephews, Chanelle,' said Maria. 'This is baby Euan and my other son, Luke. Say hello to your aunty, Luke.'

They were so cute but it was a lot to take in. Suddenly, I had two sisters and my own nephews! My brain felt like it was spinning.

'Hi, Luke,' I managed. 'How old are you then?'

He was more engrossed in his toys than talking to his new

aunty, so we all sat down. It was lovely to hear all about their lives and I felt a surge of empathy for Maria and Melissa as they recounted the pain of having me taken away from them.

Melissa said she'd been in bits when I went into foster care. 'I had to cope first with losing our mum and then you, all in a short space of time,' she said.

God knows how shattering it must have been for them both and Maria told me, 'Every time I passed a little girl in the street, I'd check if it was you.'

As for their memories of me as their new-born sister, Melissa said I was a very content baby. One of her most vivid memories of me was when our mum asked her to check on me and she said I was just lying in my cot gurgling, wriggling my hands and feet but not making any noise at all.

They were both so emotional at that meeting and I was unbelievably touched but I felt so guilty that I wasn't in floods of tears too. You see long-lost relatives meeting up on TV on shows like *Surprise, Surprise* and it's like, 'Wow! I've dreamed of meeting you all my life! I'm so happy we've found each other!' But in reality, it churns up a lot of painful memories and sentiments that are hard to handle.

Later, when I got home, Mum and Dad asked me how it went. I was still trying to process the whole encounter and said, 'Yeah, it was nice – but I feel bad that I wasn't more upset too.'

'That's understandable, Chanelle,' Mum said. 'You were only a tiny baby when you were split up and you didn't know any different. So of course, coming together again was going to affect them more. They'll understand that though.'

Mum and Dad were both so generous in how they dealt with it all. It can't have been easy for them to see me, who they'd raised as their own, swan off to meet these new relatives. I'd always felt so loyal to Mum, Dad and David, so the fact that I now had another family racked me with guilt. But, as I wrestled with these feelings, I had no idea that fate would deal us yet another cruel twist in the coming weeks.

CHAPTER TEN

Old Habits

With recent events constantly running through my mind like it was stuck on a loop, I made the bad move of turning back to Scott. He was now renting a terraced house in Wakefield and begged me to move in with him.

'This is a new start for us, babe,' he urged. 'You've dealt with all your family stuff and I've cleaned myself up and got this place. Come on, let's try living together properly. Just you and me. What do you say?'

With my head a bit of a mess, I agreed. And my parents were obviously deeply unhappy about it.

'You will regret it, trust me,' Dad warned. 'He's bad news.'

Of course, I didn't listen though and off I went. In fairness, Scott had got himself off the drugs but, within a few days, he became as controlling as ever. He'd say things like, 'Why've you got your hair like that? It looks really trampy.'

He was critical of my clothes too. 'Why are you wearing those tight jeans? You look like a tart.'

Of course, I should have told him where to go but, because I'd had such a hard time at home in the past year, I craved my independence and being with him gave me that. I was so desperate to keep him happy, even if that meant taking his constant abuse. He tried to stop me from going to school at all and then he didn't even want me to leave the house. A simple trip to the shops would result in the Spanish Inquisition.

'Where are you going? Who are you going with? What time will you be back?' he'd ask.

Worst of all, he told me that I was fat and ugly. 'You need to work out more,' he said, looking me up and down as I dressed up for a night out.

I suppose it was a tactic to make me wear clothes that covered up more of my body. Were we living in the Dark Ages or something? I really can't explain why I didn't walk out straight away but, as my self-esteem was shot to pieces, his approval meant everything. So on the rare days he was kind to me, or said, 'You look gorgeous today,' I felt thrilled. I just wanted him to love me, plain and simple.

The turning point came just before my 16th birthday. I'd planned a small party with some friends and had bought a slinky new black halter-neck dress, which I couldn't wait to wear. About a week before the big day, I was trying it on in front of the mirror and deciding what shoes to wear with it when Scott came home in a really odd mood. Despite his promises that he'd cleaned up his act, I instantly recognised that he was drugged up again, God only knows what on. And though I may have taken some crap from him over the months, whenever I sensed he'd been messing with drugs, I put my foot down, big time.

'You can't just go out taking that shit, Scott. It's not fair on me,' I snapped, as he stood staring at me, spaced out.

'If you want me to live with you, you can't do this to me, I've told you before. Don't you think knowing my mum was a drug addict is enough for me to deal with?'

But Scott seemed not to care about my feelings at all and it suddenly became as clear as day that he was never going to change for me.

With a sly smile on his face, he lurched towards me and said with a sneer, 'It's none of your business what I've been doing. But here's something you need to know. You are not wearing that dress for your party. You look like a complete slut.'

'Well, I'm sorry,' I replied, 'but I am wearing it. You can't tell me what to do.'

And then, from out of nowhere, he exploded in a fit of rage. 'Don't you dare back-chat me, you little bitch!'

Feeling scared, I tried to run out of the bedroom but he blocked my path and pushed me backwards. Now I erupted too.

'Don't fucking push me!' I shouted at the top of my lungs.

'And don't you swear at me!' he roared.

I was screaming at him to let me go and tried to shove him back but then, in one swift motion, he pushed me to the floor really hard.

'You bastard!' I shrieked, as a flash of pain jolt through my body. I picked myself up and tried to run past him again but he grabbed my hair and started pulling me down the stairs. I clung on to the banister as tightly as I could but he was too strong. As I slipped down the steps one by one, I felt the carpet stinging my skin and, the more I fought him, the more it hurt.

'Let me go!' I kept yelling and then, managing to wriggle free, I ran into the kitchen, desperate to get away from him. He followed me, calling me all sorts of awful names.

'Shut up! Shut up! Let me go! I'm not listening to this bullshit any more!'

I put my hands over my ears and tried to push him away

but he came right at me and, for a split second, I thought he was about to reach for a knife in the wooden block on the work surface.

'You're not fucking going anywhere!' he said slowly. All of a sudden, I felt my life was actually in danger. But, thank God, the neighbours had heard all the commotion and at that moment banged on the front door.

'What's going on in there?' they shouted through the letterbox. 'We've called the police.'

Scott froze in his tracks, looked me straight in the eyes and, as he realised what he'd done, his anger seemed to dissipate in an instant. He walked silently away from me and into the lounge. I opened the front door and, after convincing our neighbours I was fine, ran up to the bathroom to bathe my face. Looking in the mirror, I couldn't believe the state of what was reflected back at me. I was so young – what the hell was I doing being shoved around and listening to that kind of abuse? I should have been out having a laugh with my mates, not having a full-on domestic like some battered wife.

The police arrived a few minutes later and, as you'd expect, Scott was adamant he'd done nothing wrong.

'I would never hurt her,' he told them. 'She attacked me and I was acting in self-defence.'

I got my things together and as I left, an overwhelming sadness swept over me. I felt sorry for him for a split second but it was fleeting – I knew it was over.

Not wanting to be on my own that night, I went back to my mum and dad's – thank goodness they always kept my bedroom for me. Fortunately, they were asleep when I got home and I was so dazed I didn't want to wake them to tell them what had gone on.

The next day, after a fitful sleep, I had several bruises from our tussle and my eyes were all swollen from crying. Walking into the kitchen sheepishly, I announced myself tearfully to Mum and Dad. 'Hello. I'm back.'

'Good God! What has happened to you?' Mum said. 'You look awful.'

Dad jumped up from his seat. 'What the hell's been going on?'

'It's OK, Dad. Scott and I had a fight last night. But I'm fine.'

I told them the full story and Dad just looked and sounded so sad.

'Surely now you can see that he's no good for you, Chanelle? What's it going to take for you to see sense?'

'Don't worry. I think I've finally seen the light,' I said.

That morning, I dragged myself to school, feeling incredibly sorry for myself. Although I'd caked make-up on, I still looked rough and everyone kept asking me what had happened to me. Of course, I was too proud to admit what had really gone on. But unbelievably, Scott came to pick me up from school that day as if nothing had happened.

'Hi babe,' he said casually, as he approached me at the gates.

'What the hell are you doing here?' I seethed, barging past him. 'I don't want to see you ever again. Get lost!'

But he'd obviously planned his speech carefully. 'Chanelle, I'm so sorry. Please forgive me, I'll never do it again, I swear on my life. Please, just give me one more chance.'

'Scott, how could you be like that to me?' I shook my head. 'I can't get back with you. It's over.'

'I only got angry because I love you so much,' he said. 'But I'm going to change for you this time. It will never happen again. I swear. Please, don't throw away what we've got. We're good, you and me. And you know we are.'

A flicker of hesitation must have crossed my face because he smiled at me.

'Come on. What can I do to make it up you? Let me take you shopping and buy you a lovely birthday present.'

I still don't know why he had such a hold over me but he always knew exactly how to butter me up. Classic bullying tactics, I guess.

'I can't make any decision right now,' I said and sighed. 'I need to think about this. You've hurt me badly so many times.'

I knew in my heart that getting back with him would be the wrong thing to do but he had the ability to make me question every single thought process and decision I ever made. 'Was it all my fault?' I wondered. 'Perhaps my clothes *are* too tarty? If I hadn't bought that bloody dress, maybe it would never have happened.'

I was in such a quandary and I clearly couldn't ask my parents for guidance. I knew their take on it and that they'd be livid if they knew I was questioning things again.

Scott continued to call me constantly. And though I wouldn't talk to him, I decided to phone his mum Lynne for advice. What she said finally gave me the push I needed.

'I care about you as if you were my own daughter, Chanelle. You need to think very carefully about your future and, though it pains me to say this, I don't think it should be with Scott.'

I was shocked. 'Do you really think that badly of him?'

'Well, of course I love him, he's my son and I'll always look out for him. But I can't sit back and watch you throw away your life. I've seen you hurt so many times now and enough is enough.'

'You don't think he will change then?'

'He needs to grow up and, until he does that, you will be better off without him. Get yourself out of it. That's my best advice.'

Lynne's words deeply affected me and helped me realise that it was definitely over – for good. I had to walk away, for the sake of my own sanity.

CHAPTER ELEVEN

Sweet 16

To Mum and Dad's credit, they spared me the whole 'We told you so' act and seemed happy enough not to discuss my poor judgement over Scott.

'I don't want to talk about him ever again,' I said. 'As far as I'm concerned, it's finished.'

'Fair enough,' Mum said. 'But, please, will you just choose your next boyfriend more carefully, for all our sakes?'

'Don't worry, Mum. I will never let any guy treat me so badly again. This is the new, improved, non-doormat Chanelle,' I joked.

Well, it seemed so good in theory.

Though still hurting about the whole sorry situation, I focused all my energy on the party for my 16th and it was a really great night. In a good 'up yours' to Scott, I proudly wore the new black dress to a brilliantly cheesy club in Wakefield called Grand Central.

'You look sensational,' my friends told me. 'Screw that loser, huh?'

I felt happy for the first time in ages and knew they were right. I was worth far more than the way he'd made me feel.

Getting merry on cocktails and champagne, I felt a heavy load lift off my shoulders. I know, at 16, I wasn't really old enough to be boozing but it was all harmless enough – and way better than going out and getting wasted on ecstasy or horrible stuff like that. Anyway, as we all danced and had a good laugh, a guy called Nick, who I'd met at a mate's party a while before, sidled up to me.

'Happy birthday, gorgeous,' he said, holding his drink up to mine.

'Thanks,' I replied as we clinked glasses.

After a slightly awkward drunken pause, he garbled, 'So can I take you for a drink sometime?'

Fuelled by the booze, I giggled and gave him a hug. 'Yeah, why not?' I said. 'You know I've just come out of a relationship, so I'm not looking for anything serious but, if you're cool with that, let's have some fun.'

'Sure,' he said and grinned.

Freed from the shackles of Scott, I saw that Nick was quite cute, with highlighted hair and dark eyes. We'd been messaging each other occasionally on MySpace after meeting a few months back and he'd seemed nice and really funny.

But after we'd arranged to meet a few days later, I thought twice about it and almost called it off.

Mum told me to relax. 'You're young, you're single and you're free, Chanelle. It's only a drink, isn't it?'

Frankly, I think she was just hoping it would deter me from picking up the phone to Scott again but she was right, of course. He seemed decent enough and I could do whatever I damn well liked now.

So we met for a drink and, despite being nervous as hell, like I always am on first dates, we had a lovely evening. We just chatted for hours and began texting each other loads after that. We quickly became an item but I didn't want anything heavy or complicated, just to have a good laugh. And that's exactly what Nick gave me. Even when I was feeling low, he could make me cry with laughter and he never judged me or my past. It was nice to have an easy relationship without 50 tons of baggage attached to it.

I've got nothing bad to say about Nick at all – especially as he was there for me throughout the next traumatic experience that life decided to throw my way.

In the month or so since I'd met them, I'd been in regular touch with my new family: we'd had a barbecue at Nan's place and I'd gone to Alton Towers with Maria and Melissa. Though she seemed increasingly frail each time I saw her, it clearly made Nan so happy to see her three granddaughters bonding after all this time.

But, while I did grow close to my sisters, my feelings of guilt were still lurking, not least because I'd had a fairly privileged life after being adopted. When our mum died, Maria went to live on a rough estate in Sheffield with her dad and Melissa grew up on another tough estate in Huddersfield with her dad. On the other hand, I had a 'two-point-four-children' kind of upbringing in an affluent bit of Wakefield, with a nice house and a good education. I just got lucky, I guess.

Though I couldn't share in their memories, I did like hearing all their lovely stories about our mum because she was a real homebody before it all went so wrong. She had fallen into the destructive drug circle precisely because she wanted to put food on the table and get us a new house and her biggest wish was for the four of us to all live together.

'The biggest tragedy is that she died while trying to get her life back on track,' Melissa said.

I also learned that reading was our mum's big passion and that she used to throw big bonfire and Halloween parties at home.

And at Easter, she would fill the living room with dozens and dozens of chocolate eggs, which my sisters adored. They both said nobody ever had a bad word to say about her. Of course, it was reassuring to hear these things but it still makes me sad I wasn't a part of it. I found it hard to talk about her death too. While they would cry and cry about it, it was a bit remote to me, like an episode of *CSI*.

Meanwhile, my Nan – who Melissa and Maria always called 'Nanan' – seemed to dwell on the past a little less, perhaps because her memory wasn't as sharp by this point. I had very quickly grown extremely fond of her so, when Maria called me with some terrible news one day, I was distraught.

'Nanan's had a stroke, Chanelle,' she said. 'She's in a bad way. Apparently she can't even talk.'

This was bad. She'd already had one stroke previously, so I dropped everything and went straight to Maria's place.

'Will she pull through?' I asked them on the way to the hospital.

'No idea,' Melissa replied grimly. 'She's pretty old now, you know.'

She wasn't wrong. Nan was in her mid-eighties but looked even older and incredibly weak in her hospital bed.

Because the latest stroke had left her unable to talk, she had to write messages to us on a piece of paper. Her writing was like a child's and took a huge amount of effort, the poor thing. At one point, she scrawled, 'I'm going home on Saturday.'

'Bless her,' I thought. 'She really thinks she's well enough to leave here.'

Then, that very Saturday, a horribly spooky thing happened. It was early in the morning and I got a call from my sisters. They were both crying hysterically down the phone.

'What's the matter?' I asked, fearing the worst. 'Is it Nan?'

'She's dead,' sobbed Maria.

I almost dropped the phone. It was so horrible. She had seemed so determined to go home when we visited her but it was almost as if she had predicted her own death instead.

'What do we do now?' I said.

'We have to sort the funeral,' Maria replied, her voice shaking. 'We'll keep you posted on all the details.'

And with that, the conversation was over. There was nothing else to say. It seemed so cruel that I'd known her only a few weeks. I was not ready to have her snatched away from me so soon.

A little bit later, my tears arrived. I was despondent that I hadn't carved out more opportunities to see her but I didn't drive then and Sheffield was two train rides away. Plus I was working hard at college and part time every weekend. Somehow, those excuses didn't make me feel any better though.

The day of Nan's funeral came and, thankfully, Nick came with me. But I couldn't stop crying from the moment we arrived at the church – especially when one of the mourners came up to me and said, 'You know, Annie was hanging on until she'd met you. Now she'd finally done that, she felt it was her time to go.' That just set me off big time. The thought of her clinging to life for as long as possible until she met me was too upsetting to bear.

After the ceremony, there was a wake and my sisters and I ended up drinking far too much.

As I sat sobbing in the pub, Melissa said, 'Think about how I feel – Nanan was like a mum to me.' Maybe I was being over-sensitive because I'd had too much wine but it felt like she was telling me I couldn't grieve because I hadn't known her long enough.

'Not everything is about you, Melissa!' I snapped and we ended up having a huge row, right there in front of everyone. We were making such a scene that Maria ordered us back to her house, where the argument continued at full throttle.

'There are three of us here, you know,' I told Melissa. 'Yeah, it's bad for you but I didn't even have the chance to know her. Think how that makes me feel!'

'Shut up! You don't understand at all,' she shouted. 'How can you know? You'll never realise what we've lost.'

I'm appalled to confess to this but we then started slapping each other. It was horrific. I've never been in a physical fight in my life but that's how upset we both were.

'I wish I'd never met you!' I yelled at her, which, of course, wasn't true at all but it was the most hurtful thing I could think of to say.

'Why don't you just clear off back to your cosy little life then?'

Fortunately, someone intervened and pulled us apart and Nick then took me home.

'Don't do this to yourself,' he said, stroking my hair. 'After everything you've been through, why turn on each other like this?'

Looking back on it, while Nan had brought me and my sisters together initially, it was as if the glue couldn't hold us together after she died. I didn't speak to either of them for months after the funeral, which is so sad when we could probably have helped each other with our loss.

Eventually, we did reconcile and move on and, nowadays, I love them both dearly. I feel so grateful that they came in to my life when they did – but I will always be filled with profound regret that the three of us didn't have longer with Nan.

As I mentioned, Nick was a rock for me during that time but I knew I had to pull myself together because my GCSEs were looming that spring. It wasn't the best time to be facing big exams that would shape my future career but I threw myself into my revision for the next few months and did better than I ever could have hoped, getting all As and Bs, and even four A* grades. I was so happy that all that hard work paid off.

As a reward to myself, and probably in direct response to the heartache of the past year, I went a little crazy that summer. Nick, our friends and I would hit the bars and clubs in Wakefield most evenings and I lost count of the number of messy nights we had. I remember wearing some truly shocking outfits too, such as string vests and a coloured bra underneath, with tight pedal-pusher combats and pointy heels. I even wore sweatbands and ankle warmers – nice!

Things with Nick were going well too. Although my parents liked him, he was never allowed to stay at ours, so I spent most of my time at his house, and his parents, Vicky and Tony, became like family to me. On a Friday night, they would have friends round for dinner and drinks and there was always laughter in the house. It was just a welcoming, relaxing place to hang out.

My great exam results meant that I won a place at Greenhead College in Huddersfield that autumn, which was one of the best in the country. It's so prestigious that you have to have formal interviews to get in, so I was thrilled and very excited when they accepted me.

And, of course, Mum and Dad were so proud they could hardly get their heads through the front door for a couple of weeks after they found out! I opted to take A Levels in English, Spanish and Music and it started off brilliantly. I had a feeling this was going to be a really great time in my life.

But sadly, despite loving my subjects individually, my enjoyment of college didn't last long, thanks to my horrible Spanish teacher. For some reason, she took an instant dislike to me and was always really mean about the fact I chose to dress like Victoria Beckham.

It was 2003 and, though the Spice Girls had gone their separate ways three years earlier, my obsession with Posh was still going strong. By this point, she was doing her solo music stuff and I loved her hip-hop sound and cool new image. She did a song called 'Let Your Head Go', which turned out to be her last solo single. The video was amazing – she was sitting on a throne and wearing a tiara, then basically going mental, flinging clothes around and chucking vases of flowers with all this wild hair. She even did a mock flash of her boobs to the paparazzi before being led away by men in white coats. I loved the way Victoria could take the mickey out of herself and, though she obviously wasn't the greatest singer to have ever graced the earth, she always looked gorgeous.

As a hobby, Posh was a costly one: I spent a small fortune trying to keep up with her ever-changing wardrobe. Just as well then that I had not one but two part-time jobs during college – one at River Island and one at Cedar Court, the hotel where I still did waitressing. It was hard work but it had to be done if I wanted to wear Victoria's Rock & Republic jeans! In fact, hers was the only denim brand I'd wear and one of the worst lies I ever told Mum was that I needed to borrow £400 for one of my closest friends Rachel, who I'd met working at River Island. I told Mum I had to help her pay for a lip operation, when, in fact, it was to buy myself new jeans!

'Rachel really needs the surgery, Mum,' I fibbed. 'She's really miserable and depressed, so I've got to give her the cash.'

Mum, of course, being the kindly soul she is, handed the money over and off I went to get my VBs! I confessed all eventually and paid her back every penny but how awful was that?

Victoria also once had an amazing fake-fur bag, which had a diamante fastening on the side, and I was thrilled when I found a great high-street copy of it – for hundreds of pounds less than her designer version, obviously. But the Monday after I bought it and proudly swanned into college with it for the first time, my Spanish teacher took one look at it and said, 'You are not bringing that bag inside this classroom.'

'Why not?' I asked, innocently. 'It's like Victoria Beckham's – it's stunning.'

'It's revolting,' she replied, totally deadpan. 'Fur is disgusting, whether it's fake or not.'

'But I'm not just going to leave my bag outside class, am I?' I said, getting annoyed.

'OK, fine. Stay outside then, with your bag,' she said, smirking.

So the nasty woman then made me carry my desk out of the classroom and work in the corridor for the rest of the lesson. Have you ever heard anything so ridiculous? And as if that wasn't humiliating enough, she gave me a dressing-down in front of the whole class, saying, 'You're clearly very insecure if you think you need to look like someone else. Maybe you should stop being so pretentious.' I didn't actually understand what she meant by the word 'pretentious' but it was still like a slap in the face. I looked it up in the dictionary later and couldn't believe she had been so rude. I was doing nothing wrong and it was no different to other girls copying any trend off the catwalk. I mean, the whole thing was crazy; the bag wasn't even real! I don't agree with killing animals either but this was a fake from a high-street shop that all girls my age went to.

That pretty much set our relationship in stone and, as anyone close to me will tell you, when I develop a grudge against someone, it goes deep.

From then on, it was all-out war between us. She made me cry several times and actually called me a bimbo in front of the whole class! That was a ridiculous accusation because I wore mainly jeans and vest tops to college and would never have dreamed of turning up in a tiny skirt like some of the other girls in my year. I hated the whole trashy Paris Hilton look and thought Victoria's style was much more sophisticated. But for some reason, because I liked to look after my appearance and always had nice make-up, manicured nails and a matching bag, this silly woman seemed to think I was some brain-dead slapper.

I never really got what her problem was. Especially as most people thought my worship of Posh was vaguely amusing. And you know what? Her blatant dislike of me only encouraged me to annoy her as much as I possibly could. So I'd try to copy as many of Victoria's looks as possible, tearing out pictures from magazines and searching for similar clothes on the high street. I loved the way she'd make a simple jumper dress with a belt or a granddad shirt look so effortlessly cool.

And, as you'll soon find out, my obsession with Posh was soon to hit a whole new level.

CHAPTER TWELVE

a Dream Come True

I know I shouldn't have let it get to me but my problems with my Spanish teacher at Greenhead tarnished my whole college experience. Before that, I had always been the teachers' favourite at school, so this felt a bit like rejection. I hated it. I'll also admit that, because this was such a brilliant college, I was only an average student there, which made me stop working as hard. I know it's ridiculous and makes me sound very spoiled but I thought, 'What's the point in even staying here?'

After dropping out towards the end of my first term, I got a full-time job at a call centre with Halifax bank and was also waitressing at Oulton Hall Hotel, near Leeds. Hardly the road to academic glory that I had planned to pursue but at least I was earning decent money. My parents were obviously disappointed, as I'd worked so hard to earn a place at Greenhead, but they didn't want me to be miserable either. And they perked up when I started my A Levels again at New College in Pontefract that September – which was a much better choice for me. For starters, my Spanish teacher there, Lola, was absolutely lovely, so I happily got back into my studies.

That year, there was a major item on my to-do list: I was desperate to learn to drive and get my own car, so I could be more independent. My only way of doing this was to borrow the money from my parents, so I made a detailed financial plan, which I presented to Dad. I thought it was so grown up because it showed all my incomings and outgoings and how long it would take me to pay them back the £3,500 I'd estimated I needed. I gave him this sheet of A4 paper with all my mathematical scribblings on it and I'd written at the bottom:

Love you, Daddy, and with this car I can't go out getting drunk apart from once a month so I will study more + be really intelligent and get a great job.

Please, Dad, this would make me really happy and prove to you I'm responsible, I just need help to get on the ladder! xxx (I won't let you down!)

How could he resist that? Even though I was generally such a pain in the arse, he got me the car, which was so sweet. Then I started driving lessons with this fantastic woman called Anne, who had the patience of a saint. But on the odd occasion my dad did take me out for a practice, we'd end up pulling over at the side of the road screaming at each other and then he'd drive us home. Still, I passed first time, so I can't have been that bad.

Having my own car made life so much easier when I was going to and from college in Pontefract every day, plus juggling two part-time jobs at the same time – and I saved a fortune on bus fares! Overall, I was very happy at Pontefract but it was around this time when I realised that Nick and I were starting to drift apart. Don't get me wrong, we still got on so well but our goals in life were poles apart. He was drifting along, working as a lifeguard at a local pool, which was fine for him, but I felt he lacked drive. It sounds cruel and I don't mean it to but I've always been headstrong and had lots of big aims and plans for the future. Ambition is one of the things I admire most in men – I think Simon Cowell should be everyone's role model! It's not that I fancy him (he'd be far too old for me) but I love the fact he came from a normal background and has got to the amazing heights he's at now. It's not about money either; the determination to succeed is what attracts me to someone. I just think Simon's brilliant. I'd give my house to meet him!

Anyway, there was no big scene between Nick and me but, as I was looking ahead to my eighteenth birthday that November, it became clear that our two-year relationship was over. We'd booked a holiday to the Dominican Republic but, just before we were about to go, I backed out – even though it had cost us £1,000 each.

'Nick,' I said as we sat side by side on the couch. 'You know I love you, don't you?'

'Er, yes, I guess I do.'

'And that I'll always love you?'

'Uh-huh.'

'Well, I think I've grown to love you as my friend, rather than my boyfriend. Does that make sense?'

'It does actually, yes.'

'Do you hate me for saying it?'

'Massively. I don't think I'll ever talk to you again.'

'Are you being serious? Don't wind me up, Nick.'

'No, it's OK, really. I've kind of been thinking the same thing.'

'Honestly?'

'Yeah, I think we've just sort of moved on, haven't we?'

'So, for the record, are we splitting up?'

'Looks like it, doesn't it?'

'Well,' I said and smiled, 'can we be official best friends from now on then?'

'Seeing as you put it so nicely, there's nobody I'd rather be best mates with.'

And as he gave me a playful punch on the arm, that was it. We were through. Talk about the smoothest break-up in history. No blazing rows, no fighting over possessions, no tears. How civilised! If only my love life could always have been such a breeze.

Being single again not only allowed me to concentrate more on my studies but also on the other super-important thing in my life: Victoria Beckham! I think it's fair to say that this was the year my Posh obsession went sky high.

I still made lots of effort to dress like her but the one thing that had always been difficult for me to copy was her long, luscious hair extensions because they were so ridiculously expensive. One time, I raided £2,000 from a savings account that Mum and Dad had set up for me, just to pay for some. Unsurprisingly, they weren't over the moon when they found out the hard-earned cash they'd stashed away for my future had gone towards paying for some poor eastern-European girl's cast-offs to weave into my own hair.

'That was our little nest egg for you,' said Mum sadly. 'And now there's nothing.'

God, I felt terrible. Sorry again, Mum and Dad!

However, there were no such hair challenges when Victoria very helpfully cut her hair short into a drastic bob. I was thrilled – this look was going to be a cinch to replicate! So I marched straight down to my hairdressers, saying, 'Give me a Pob, please, right now!'

That haircut made me look even more like her and people on the street would often stop and do a double-take, especially if I was wearing big sunnies and my VB jeans. You can imagine how ecstatic I was when people pointed out my likeness to her. It began happening frequently whenever I glammed up for a night out and I bloody loved it! I even started posing like her and pouting, which Zoe, Alison and co. thought was hilarious! Somebody telling me 'You look like Victoria Beckham,' was the ultimate compliment and always gave me a real high. It might seem daft now but so what? Who was I harming?

A lot of people have asked me over the years what I made of the whole Rebecca Loos scandal and how I could still hold the Beckhams up as role models after David reportedly cheated on Victoria while he was playing for Real Madrid in 2004. Well, I'll admit I was mortified when all that came out but I flatly refused to believe it and would say to everyone, 'No, Victoria's denied it. Trust me, it didn't happen.'

But whatever did or didn't go on in Spain, that desperado Rebecca still makes me sick to this day. I remember a few years back, I was meant to be doing a shoot for the *Daily Star* and I heard that she was going to be there the same day doing some pictures. So I phoned in and said, 'I'm not coming in – I refuse to be in the same studio as that tramp!'

While I stayed loyal to the Beckhams through and through, one thing still eluded me. I had never met Victoria and I knew I wouldn't truly feel satisfied in life until I'd managed to arrange that little feat.

After putting her pop career to one side, Victoria had, by now, established herself as a designer and published a lovely glossy fashion book called *That Extra Half An Inch*. And when I heard she was going to be signing copies at Selfridges in London, it became my life's mission to see her in the flesh once and for all.

I had to take the day off college for it and convinced my friend Jamila – who I'd met at Halifax – to come with me. We drove all the way down from Wakefield, which I remember was particularly scary as it was the first time I'd driven to London since passing my test. Along with 3,000 other fans, we stood in this never-ending queue for hours but I'd have happily stood there for a week just to meet her. As we inched nearer and nearer to Victoria, I was so nervous I thought I was going to black out. I still remember it like it was yesterday – she was wearing a lovely black dress with black tights and stilettos, and was impossibly tiny. I recall thinking she looked like a little ant, albeit a very beautiful one! And contrary to what people always say about her being miserable and cold, she was smiling loads too and seemed very warm. As we finally reached the front of that queue, I basically turned to mush. I never normally get starstruck or lost for words but I just couldn't think of anything to say. All words vanished from my head as she signed my copy of the book and I blurted out, 'People say that I really look like you.'

What a cringe-worthy thing to say! But, to this day, I still can't believe her reply. Looking up from the book and taking me in with her big brown eyes, she smiled and said, 'Well, that's a huge compliment to me.'

No effing way! To be told I was good looking by Victoria Beckham was literally the best thing anyone had ever said to me. It really was one of the greatest moments of my life. I went home on cloud nine and stayed up there for several days.

I know people thought I was a bit strange but my adulation of Victoria was all so innocent. Surely it's no different to being a One Direction fan nowadays – although I never stalked Victoria or tried to break into her hotel room! But just in case you're wondering, I do still love the Beckhams today. When I see cute pictures of David cuddling and kissing their toddler Harper, I totally melt. There simply can't be any better father figure in the public eye. They do everything for their kids and they always have. Regardless of what people think of me and the choices I've made in my life, those are exactly my values.

Overall, I have a lot to thank Posh for. If I hadn't looked a bit like her, I would never have got any of the opportunities that later came my way. So Victoria, on the off-chance that you're reading this, I'm eternally grateful to you!

CHAPTER THIRTEEN

Head Over Heels

Your 18th birthday is meant to be one of the most memorable occasions of your life, isn't it? Well, in typical Chanelle style, mine didn't quite go according to plan!

Mum and I had organised a huge party for loads of family and friends for the Saturday my big day fell on and she had even made me the same birthday cake Victoria Beckham once had, which was in the shape of a Muller Lite yoghurt pot with fruit on the side. On the Friday night, I'd been planning a quiet evening at home to prepare my liver but Rachel suggested we went for a quick drink in the pub after our shift at River Island finished. It really was only meant to be a swift one – we were still in our highly attractive uniforms, after all! We used to pop into this pub regularly after work and would always order a glass of Liebfraumilch. We thought we were so sophisticated – ha!

Even though I can't stand the stuff now, we bought a whole bottle that evening and sat there getting really hammered. Later, we ended up going to the roughest club possible, in Dewsbury, called Frontier, and we just had the best night ever, dancing, drinking and laughing. It was one of those unplanned occasions that just turns out all the better because it's so spontaneous. But then, on my actual birthday the next day, we woke up at separate ends of my little single bed, with a greasy half-eaten cheeseburger lying next to my face on the pillow and Rachel cuddling the remnants of a kebab! We felt so unbelievably rough at my party. Everyone had made such a massive effort and there we were drinking lemonade. Oh dear.

Over the next few months, I got my head down at college and started a new part-time job in a bar called Tryst, in Wakefield. And one Saturday night, I experienced one of those real thunderbolt moments as I clapped eyes on the most gorgeous guy I'd seen in ages.

His name was Ian and he was tall, dark and unbelievably fit. But, boy, did he know it! He was one of those guys who worked the room with his eyes, knowing he could have any girl he liked. His brazen confidence (and buff body!) reeled me in straight away.

'All right, gorgeous?' he said, winking at me as I served him a drink. Bingo! 'Has anyone ever told you that you look like Victoria Beckham? Except you're more foxy!' Double, triple bingo!

Funnily enough, I was wearing a pair of VB jeans, which I quickly pointed out.

'Very nice,' he said and nodded, checking out my bum.

By some small stroke of luck, Ian was mates with Rachel's boyfriend, which provided the perfect excuse for us to be introduced.

'Lovely to meet you,' he said with a grin and I felt my face flush like some kid in the playground.

'You too,' I said, smiling back and praying that my hair hadn't gone disgustingly flat in the heat of the bar.

'What time does your shift finish?' he asked. 'Fancy joining us for a drink later?'

'Mmm, fast worker!' I thought. But he definitely liked me. Result!

'Oh, I'm working until closing time,' I said, silently cursing. 'And I'd better get back to it or I'll get the sack.'

'Well, can I take your number?' he asked. 'Let's hook up another time.'

I always try to act coyly when I first meet a guy I like but who was I kidding here? He was seriously hot and this was butterflies-in-the-stomach territory. I gave him my number and spent the rest of the night trying not to look at him every five seconds. Whenever I did catch his eye though, I felt a bit giddy.

'When am I taking you for dinner then?' he texted late that night.

Screw my rule about not wanting to seem too keen.

'How about tomorrow?' I replied.

He took me for a pizza and it felt like we'd known each other years. He was so charming and we didn't stop laughing the entire time.

'I think this could be the start of something good,' he told me when he dropped me home. And before I had the chance to reply, he gave me a slow, lingering kiss, which quite literally left me breathless.

I floated off to sleep that night and, when I switched my phone on the next morning, a text beeped in. It said, 'Thanks for the best night. You're not only beautiful but loads of fun too. Can't wait to see you again.'

From that moment on, we were inseparable and, though Rachel was quick to warn me that he was a bit of a player, I laughed it off.

'Ian's never been with a girl for more than a couple of weeks,' she said. 'So, please, be careful.'

'Yeah, yeah,' I assured her. 'Thanks for your concern but he honestly doesn't seem that type at all.'

Aged 23 to my 18, he was more mature than most guys I'd met and he didn't mind when I announced that I was going to call him by his middle name, Spencer, instead of Ian – just because I liked it.

One weekend soon after, I was meant to be going away with Mum, Dad and David to Center Parcs but I spotted an opportunity that was too tempting to pass up.

'I'm really sorry,' I told them. 'But I can't get the time off from the call centre this weekend after all. And I'm so tired, I think I'm just going to crash here instead.'

They didn't suspect a thing and merely said, 'Behave yourself,' as they left on Friday.

'Of course,' I said and laughed, as I secretly plotted my first evening at home with Spencer.

At the last minute, Becca, a really close friend I'd met while working at Cedar Court, begged me to have a quick drink with her because she was going off to South Africa the next day.

'OK,' I said. 'But I can't stay long. Spencer's coming over tonight and I am beyond excited!'

When he arrived, I was putting on some make-up and he gave me a puzzled look.

'Are we going out?' he said. 'I thought we were staying in?'

'You're staying here. I'm nipping out for a farewell drink with Becca but I'll be back in an hour. Is that OK?'

'Sure,' he said. 'I'll just watch TV, cook dinner and make myself at home.'

In the end, I stumbled in at 2am, blind drunk, which was really lame of me. Instead of the night of passion I'd envisaged, I conked out on the living-room floor, slurring, 'I want to watch *Ice Age*,' over and again. What an idiot!

I felt dreadful the next morning but Spencer was lovely about it, despite the ruined meal. With a sore head, I headed to work while Spencer stayed at home. And when I got back that evening, I was stunned to find that he'd cleaned the whole place from top to bottom and made me dinner again.

'Are you for real?' I asked him. 'What's the catch?'

'Er, there isn't one,' he said with a shrug. 'I just want to do everything I can to make you happy.'

Well, he was doing exactly that and I'm pleased to report that, on that particular evening, there was no drunken falling asleep, if you catch my drift!

This honeymoon period seemed to go on for ages and we never argued. I couldn't see why I had been warned about his reputation because he spent every single night with me, or down at the bar while I was working. For one of the few times in my life, I felt truly content with Spencer and, what's more, Mum and Dad thought he was great too.

'I've never seen you smile or laugh as much as you do now,' Mum said one day. 'I think you might end up marrying Spencer.'

'Do you reckon?' I said and laughed. I'd never given marriage any thought at all but she wasn't the only person to say this.

A little while later, Spencer sat me down and said, 'Chanelle, I've something to tell you.'

'What is it? Don't tell me: I'm dumped.'

'No! Shut up. Look, this is hard for me. I've never said it to any girl before. But I want you to know that, well, I love you. I want to spend my life with you. That's all.'

My jaw must have dropped to the ground and I had no idea what to say.

'Oh, Spencer, that's really lovely but you don't have to say it if you don't mean it,' I said, taking his hand.

'I do mean it. I wouldn't say it otherwise.'

He looked visibly hurt and I could tell he was waiting for me to tell him the same but I wasn't ready to do that just yet. I thought I did love him but, after my awful experience with Scott, I had to wait a bit longer to be absolutely sure I wouldn't get hurt again.

Early the next morning, he texted me: 'Why didn't you say you loved me back? I'm confused.' It'd obviously really got to him. So I called Becca and filled her in.

'Are you mad?' she said. 'What's holding you back? He makes you laugh, you fancy him and he's fun. He's caring and thoughtful and your family adore him. Do you need your head testing, girl?'

She was right, of course. I had nothing to be worried about.

A few days later, I cooked him a candlelit meal and, before we sat down, put my arms around him. 'I know I might not express it very well but this is just to tell you that I do love you.'

He hugged me and said, 'That means the world to me, Chanelle. I'll never forget it.'

It felt good for me to let go of the barriers I'd put up too.

After that, Spencer and I got into the habit of giving each other silly little presents. For instance, he was obsessed with brushing his teeth all the time so, every time I was in a bar or club, I'd buy him one of those little balls from the vending machine in the toilets, which contain a tiny toothbrush! It always amused him. He'd make me CDs of 'our songs' and he was forever bringing me Mars bars, which were my absolute favourite.

I know it probably all sounds a bit too perfect and I suppose we were one of those sickening loved-up couples that you'd roll your eyes at for canoodling on the bus. So that's precisely why I was so staggered when it all went so horribly and painfully wrong.

CHAPTER FOURTEEN

The Hardest Decision

The nightmare began when I got really sick all of a sudden. I kept throwing up for days and felt too terrible to even get out of bed. Spencer, who was working as a legal secretary, ducked out in his lunch hour every day to come and check on me, making sure I was eating when I could manage to. In fact, the only things I could stomach were, bizarrely, hot dogs and Cadbury's Mini-Rolls, so he was forever bringing me fresh supplies.

It seemed like I had a bad case of gastric flu but, when I was still being sick after a couple of weeks, I dragged myself to my GP, a nice lady who I got on well with.

She seemed baffled. 'Well, it can't be a bug, as they clear up after a few days,' she said. 'I think we need to do some blood tests.'

'OK,' I said forlornly. 'I just want to get well. I'm missing a lot of college work and I feel like death all the time.'

After she took a sample of blood, she added, 'I'm going to do a quick pregnancy test for you as well, so we can rule that out.'

I actually laughed out loud. 'What? You don't need to do that,

I'm on the pill – there's absolutely no way I could be pregnant.'

'Well, we need to make sure. You never know.'

You've probably guessed what happened next. She went over to the other side of the room and dipped the little stick into my urine, looked at it and then did a double-take. She got another stick and dipped it in again and then repeated it a third time.

'What? What is it? I asked. 'Don't tell me – it can't be…'

She turned around to face me and very simply said, 'Chanelle, you are pregnant.'

I swear I almost passed out. 'But that's impossible,' I protested. 'There's just no way. What about my pill? I don't believe it.'

'Look, the evidence is right here,' she said softly. 'I'm not making this up. You are expecting a baby and have been for about six weeks now.'

It only occurred to me then that I hadn't had a period the previous month. But as they've always been a bit erratic because I have polycystic ovaries, I didn't pay it any attention at all.

Although, at the time, I thought I was fairly scrupulous about taking my pill, I did occasionally forget to take it for a day. But I just assumed that one skipped day here or there wouldn't make any difference. I'm not proud of that now.

'I can't tell my boyfriend,' I said to her. 'He'll freak out. Will you call him for me?'

Fortunately, I'd been going to my doctor since I was a little girl and we'd always got on well, so she called Spencer at work for me.

'Chanelle has asked me to pass on a message to you. She feels unable to talk to you herself at the moment but it's pretty serious.' There was a pause. 'No, she's fine. But we've just done some tests here and she is pregnant.' Another long pause. 'Spencer? Are you all right? What do you want me to tell her?'

Eventually, she hung up and said, 'He wants you to go and meet him after work.'

I drifted out of the surgery in a kind of trance, feeling utterly numb. It wasn't that I was appalled by the news, I just felt unable to process what it meant for us both and our future.

I got to his office dead on 5.30pm and immediately things seemed different between us. He didn't kiss me and there was a coolness there. We went for a coffee and it was unbelievably awkward. We barely spoke and Spencer kept looking at me blankly, his normally sparkling eyes full of anxiety.

'I don't know what to say,' was all he could offer.

I was dying to hear the words, 'Don't worry, honey, we'll get through this together,' but, from the very beginning, it felt like it was my problem alone.

I could have handled it better if he'd said, 'Look, I'm just not ready to be a dad. What do you think our options are?'

That would have made sense but the fact that he wouldn't say anything or discuss his feelings at all made it doubly hard for me.

With my head all over the place, I realised the only person I'd be able to talk to about this predicament was my sister Maria, who had given birth to her son Luke when she was 18, the same age as me. That same evening, Spencer and I got the train up to her place. During the journey, we sat in total silence. It was as if a screen had suddenly come down and he was a completely different person. He sat staring out of the window and wouldn't touch me, or even look at me.

Within seconds of arriving on Maria's doorstep, I blurted tearfully, 'I'm pregnant! What are we going to do?'

'Oh God,' she said before ushering us both inside. 'How? I thought you were... OK, just calm down. Don't get upset.'

Maria was great in a crisis and, as Spencer sat silently in the corner, she said, 'You obviously have some tough choices to make. What are you thinking?'

Glancing across at Spencer, whose eyes were fixed on his feet,

I wiped my eyes and sighed. 'We, well… I haven't got a clue. I've got no idea. At the moment, I just can't get my head around the fact there's a little baby inside me.'

'It is a lot to take in,' she said and nodded. 'I remember, when I first found out I was pregnant, it took me days to accept it. Weeks even.'

She paused, then said, 'I'm not sure if I should tell you this because I don't want to push you either way but I would never, ever change anything about my decision to have Luke, you know.'

'Yeah,' I said slowly. 'I understand where you're coming from. I know how much you adore him.'

'I know I was very young but he helped make me who I am today. My life changed for the better when I had Luke, really it did.' She hesitated. 'But at the same time, if I could go back and have him a little later in life, I probably would. Being a young mum is bloody tough. I'm not going to lie.' Her eyes darted towards Spencer, who was still hunched in the chair. 'Particularly if you were ever to end up a single mum.'

There was so much to think about. Later on, after Spencer and I had got the train back to Wakefield, I started walking briskly towards the bus station for home, figuring he would follow me. Instead, he announced curtly, 'I'm not coming with you. I'm going home.'

That was virtually the first thing he'd said all evening and it got my back up.

'Fine! Be like that,' I snapped, walking away. And that was how we left things.

At home, I went straight to bed, not saying anything to my parents. How the hell could I?

I called Spencer the next morning but he didn't pick up his mobile all day. He wouldn't take my calls at work either. I kept texting too, saying, 'Please call me. Why are you avoiding me?'

Assuming he just needed some space, I called again the next day but still couldn't get hold of him. This was absolutely unbelievable. I felt so alone and was still feeling sick too, so I climbed back into bed and stayed there. After a couple of days, Mum came into my bedroom and said, 'Are you going to get up today, love? Why don't you have a nice bath and I'll make you some breakfast? That'll make you feel better.'

'No, I'm ill. Leave me alone,' I said flatly.

On the fourth day, she came in again and said, 'What's wrong with you? I thought the doctor didn't find anything the matter, so pull yourself together. You'll feel better if you get up.'

I ignored her and turned over in my bed to face the wall so she couldn't see my eyes brimming with tears.

Clearly, she just thought I'd had a huge bust-up with Spencer because he wasn't coming over any more, so I can see why she wasn't more sympathetic.

College had been phoning home too, asking where I was, and nothing got my dad angrier than the thought of me bunking off again. He barged in and shouted, 'Get up! Stop being so lazy. There's nothing wrong with you!'

Again, I said nothing and curled myself up into a little ball, pulling the duvet right over me. I was drained and had nothing to fight him with. There was a pain gnawing away at my insides that wouldn't go away.

With Mum now very concerned that I'd spent nearly a week in bed and was barely eating, she asked Becca – who was now back from South Africa – to come round and try talking to me. When she arrived, she sprinted upstairs and sat on my bed.

'Right then, you. What's up?' she asked.

I sat up and burst into tears. 'Becca, I'm pregnant. I don't know what to do!'

She went very pale and hugged me tightly.

'Shit. How far gone?'

'About six or seven weeks,' I wept.

'Do you want to keep it?'

'I do and I don't. I've been thinking about it for days and I can't make any sense of it. Spencer's fucked off and left me too. He won't even discuss it.'

'You poor, poor thing,' she said, pushing my matted hair off my face. 'Can't you tell your mum? I'm sure she'd be understanding.'

'No!' I said with a sniff. 'Promise me you won't say anything. They'll kill me. I can't say anything yet. Not until I know what I want to do.'

Becca then clicked into practical mode. 'OK,' she said. 'You're coming home with me.'

Once I was at her place, I had a long bath and we spent the whole night talking it over.

'Have you considered an abortion?' Becca said tentatively.

Because I'd had nobody to talk to, the word sounded revolting when I was suddenly confronted with it.

'Sort of but I don't think I could bear to, you know...' My words fell away.

The truth of the matter was that I kept thinking about my real mum, who wasn't much older than me when she had her children. She must have faced the same heart-wrenching decision and, though it can't have been practical for her to keep us either, she did. Whatever her situation, she still valued our lives enough to go through with it. I was lucky to be alive, so the thought of getting rid of the baby inside me was unthinkable on many levels.

On the flipside, I didn't feel anywhere near ready to keep it either. 'I'm still at college, I can barely look after myself, let alone a little baby,' I reasoned to Becca. 'How would I afford it? Where would I live?' I said, uncertain if my parents would be able – or willing – to support me.

Becca was such a brilliant listener and helped me face up to all the crunch issues. But there was still no word from Spencer and, after a couple of days, I went home again and straight back to bed. A couple of days later, Dad stormed into my room, dragging the duvet off me.

'Get your backside out of bed right now!' he fumed. 'You're not sick, there's nothing wrong at all. You're just wasting your life! Get out of bed right now!'

He grabbed my arm and tried to pull me up but I started screaming.

'Get off me, Dad! Just leave me alone! You don't understand!'

With me lashing out and kicking him, he let go.

'OK, fine,' he said, throwing his hands in the air wildly. 'But if you refuse to go into college, you can study here instead. I'm not having you doing nothing while you're in this house and that's final.'

College had been sending me work to get on with and it was piling up. But right now, it seemed totally irrelevant to me.

'Just get off my back, Dad,' I shouted. 'There are more important things in the world than my homework. Stop trying to control me!'

This really incensed him again and this time he did yank me out of bed and, with a tight grip on my arms, pulled me out of the room. I was flailing and slapping his hands, using every bit of me to try to get free of him.

Dad raged, 'You'll never amount to anything at this rate. You're a mess, you're so bloody selfish!'

'Get off me! I am sick!' I yelled back. 'Look at the colour of me and how much weight I've lost!'

That much was true. I hadn't eaten properly for a couple of weeks, so I was getting very thin. As we wrestled each other outside my bedroom door, I suddenly slipped and almost lost my footing. I clung to the banister to stop myself falling down the stairs. We both froze and Dad looked aghast. How had it come to this? I got up, grabbed my mobile phone and ran into the bathroom.

I was absolutely livid. If I had fallen down those stairs, I could have lost my baby. How dare he put me at risk like that? Of course, he had no idea that I was pregnant and was only trying to help me but I was not thinking rationally.

I still can't believe I did this but, using my mobile, I dialled 999 and told the police, 'Please come quickly. My dad just tried to throw me down the stairs!'

What a hateful thing for me to do.

Dad was hammering on the door for me to come out but I shouted back, 'I've called the police, so you might as well back off now.'

All went quiet and I sat on the edge of the bath, realising that my decision was made: I wanted to keep the baby. Fearing for the baby's safety had crystallised something in my brain. It was my duty to protect it.

Within 10 minutes, the police turned up and my poor dad was cautioned. I'm so ashamed that I did that to him and I don't think I'll ever forgive myself for the humiliation I caused him. There's no way he'd ever intentionally have hurt me, not in a million years. Whatever run-ins I've had with Dad in the past, he is a wonderful, caring man at heart. As a part-time social worker, he works with children for a living and pours his own money into a youth club, so I was completely out of line to risk wrecking his reputation like that.

As I sat feeling scared and vulnerable in my room, one of the police officers came in to talk to me and it must have been clear to them that this had been blown out of all proportion.

'What's really going on here?' she said. 'There's no sign of injury or violence. Is this just a row that got out of hand?'

Reluctantly, I said, 'Kind of. I'm sorry.'

Her face clouded and she shook her head at me. 'That's really not on. And your father is…'

Butting in, I whispered, 'Look, I can explain. It's just that, oh God… Well, the thing is, they don't know this but I'm pregnant.'

'I see,' she said, her expression softening a little.

'I called you out of panic because I was worried something might happen to the baby. But you can't tell my mum and dad. Please, they don't know about this and I don't want them to yet.'

I thought I had legal rights and that she would respect my wishes but she went downstairs and filled them in on everything.

When the police left, they both came upstairs and, in a state of shock, Mum said, 'Chanelle, the policewoman told us that you're pregnant. We need to talk about this.'

'I don't want to. Leave me alone, please,' I said, sobbing again. 'When I'm ready, we'll talk. But I need to deal with this my way.'

That night, I called Becca. 'Mum and Dad know,' I mumbled. 'What am I going to do? I think I want to keep the baby but I can't face talking to them.'

As calm as ever, she told me to get a bag of stuff together and she came to pick me up. As I left, Mum said, 'We're here whenever you need us. And whatever you decide to do, we will support you.'

I don't know why I couldn't discuss it with them and wish I had been together enough to sit down with them and go over it properly. But, as always, running away was the easier option, so I went to stay with Becca for two weeks.

During that time, with Spencer still AWOL, I decided that enough was enough and went round to his family home. Unfortunately, his dad answered the door and, giving me a look of disgust, said, 'What are you doing here? You've tried to trap my son into a lifetime of hell.'

He might as well have slapped me round the face. Too shocked to respond, I ran away from the house, tears rolling down my face. I was so confused. What had Spencer been telling them? That I had got pregnant on purpose? How could he do that?

Although I'd decided by now that I wanted to keep the baby, Spencer finally called me a few days later and what he said changed everything again.

'Hi, Chanelle,' he said brightly. 'I've been doing some thinking and I've reached a decision. I don't care if you have this baby or not but, if you do, I'll make sure everyone knows you'd be an unfit mother.'

I could not believe what I was hearing. As words refused to form in my mouth, he added, 'I'll say you can't look after a child because you're still a child yourself. The authorities take babies off young mums all the time. I'll say that your family won't be supportive and that your bedroom is too small. So if that's what you want, go ahead and have the baby. But if not, I suggest you get yourself booked into Marie Stopes pretty quickly.'

He then hung up and I immediately wondered if I'd just dreamed the entire conversation. How could this man who'd said he'd never leave me say something so poisonous?

It was only then that I realised the magnitude of my situation and that I was on my own. The prospect of a termination now loomed larger than ever. My options had shrunk in the space of two minutes and all these questions once again began flooding my mind. Could I really be a single mum? What about my studies and dream of going to university? Where would I live when the baby was born? How would I provide for us both? Did I really want to bring a child into this world who didn't have a dad?

As much as it pained me, it really did begin to feel like I had no choice at all. The idea sickened me but an abortion was my only way out of this mess. But could I go through with it?

CHAPTER FIFTEEN

To Hell and Back

I was nine weeks pregnant when I booked myself in for the abortion and it was truly the single worst thing I have ever had to do. Becca drove me to the Marie Stopes clinic and tried to convince me I was doing the right thing.

'You're an ambitious girl and you'd ruin your career before it's even started if you had a baby now,' she said.

I looked out of the window. 'Yes but do I really have the right to destroy a life because of that?'

'Come on. What kind of life would it ever have, Chanelle? You're just not ready for this.'

I couldn't reply. My eyes were filling up and it took all my concentration not to dissolve right there in the car. When we got to the clinic, I could hardly walk up the steps. Inside, the atmosphere was like a morgue. There were a few other young women in the waiting room and I wondered if they felt as lost and ashamed as I did.

'If it's a tablet, I can probably face it,' I whispered to Becca. 'It won't seem so much like I'm killing it. But if I have to be put to sleep and have it ripped out of me with a vacuum cleaner, I can't go through with it.' She squeezed my hand tightly.

When the nurse called me in, she confirmed that I could have a series of tablets to bring on a miscarriage, which I was relieved about.

But first, I begged her to show me a scan of the baby. I was still so torn about my decision that I felt like I needed to see evidence of the life inside me. Although she was reluctant for me to see the scan, I persisted and she eventually agreed. And the image confronting me on the screen made it very real all of a sudden.

'There's its heartbeat,' the nurse said. 'There it is. Do you see it?'

I did and it was absolutely gutting.

'I can't go through with this!' I wanted to scream. 'It's all just wrong!'

But I bit my tongue. Some part of me knew I had to keep calm, even though it was so hard not to lose the plot. Seeing such physical signs of the baby being alive and breathing was absolute torture.

The nurse sent me away that evening to have one last think about what I was going to do. Not surprisingly, I hardly slept a wink all night. The next morning, Becca picked me up again. 'Are we still going ahead then?' she asked me gently.

Wasn't this Spencer's job? He was the one who was meant to be holding my hand, guiding me through this agony.

'Yes, my mind is made up,' I said firmly.

Straight after I took the first tablet, Becca and I both burst into tears and clung to each other. I don't know what I'd have done without her there.

A bit later, I went into the toilet and half-heartedly tried to stick my fingers down my throat to bring it back up but nothing happened.

I had to take a few more pills when I got home and, before long, the miscarriage started. I spent the whole of the next day doubled over in agony and bleeding heavily.

It was the worst feeling I've ever experienced, knowing that my baby was being expelled from my body. It seemed so brutal and I could hardly speak in the days that followed. Becca respected my wish not to talk about it and, eventually, I returned home and broke the news to Mum and Dad.

They hugged me for a long time and Mum said, 'I would never have tried to influence you but I think you've made the right decision. It would have been different if Spencer had wanted the baby but I don't know how you would have managed alone.'

She was right, of course, but I was inconsolable about what I'd done. I woke up every day thinking, 'You're a murderer,' and genuinely hated myself. Worryingly, for the first time in a long while, I thought about killing myself again. Some days, when I was driving to work, I'd think, 'I don't deserve to be here. I might as well just drive off this bridge.'

Why not? It made sense to me – I'd killed someone. Was I really any better than my mother's murderer? Looking back, I must have been suffering from some kind of post-traumatic stress but I never saw that at the time. At my lowest, I even tried to get Spencer to come back to me. I was so shattered that it seemed like only he could fill the void that the abortion had left. I called him and said, 'Can't we put all of this behind us now and get back what we had before?'

I must have sounded so desperate and he didn't want to know.

'Stop calling me,' he said. 'I don't want to see you or speak to you. Leave me alone.'

I also grew obsessed with how my tummy looked after the abortion. I was convinced that being pregnant, even for a short time, had left me with wobbly skin. It was nonsense, of course, but I decided I had to get my stomach taut and rock-hard as a way of eradicating the evidence of what I'd done. So I started going to the gym for two hours every day, before college in the morning and then after my shift at the call centre if I was working. I'd run and run on the treadmill until I was exhausted and afterwards would go and sit in the sauna for ages to try and sweat more out of me.

Mum became so worried about my weight obsession that she hid the scales at home.

'Why are you working out so much, Chanelle?' she asked. 'You don't need to, you know. You look perfect as you are.'

She and Dad would make me eat big meals with them, so I started taking laxatives as well. The problem went beyond my weight too, as I also had my hair extensions taken out and got my hair cut really short. With my self-image in tatters, depriving myself of food was a way I could make myself feel better. On a good day, I could get away with eating just an apple and an orange and it became such an obsession that I stopped going out with my friends. Drinking would just fill me with unnecessary calories.

As well as going to the gym twice a day, I sometimes even went for a swim at the pool next to college during my lunch hour. Before long, my weight had dropped to 6st 12lbs, which was severely underweight for my height. I felt drained and exhausted all the time and, at work, I kept having to cancel calls that came in because I didn't have the energy to answer them.

One day my friend Jamila – who'd gone with me to meet Victoria Beckham – sat me down for a chat. 'Chanelle, what's going on? You look awful. Your clothes are falling off you and you're deathly pale. What's this all about?'

'I'm fine,' I lied. 'I've just been working hard and dashing around so much that I'm not eating as much as before. But you

know me, I still love my McDonalds.' That was blatantly untrue
– I was stick-thin and hadn't been near a burger in ages.

Things took a turn when I went to see my doctor and asked
her to prescribe me some slimming pills. She frowned, took a
knowing look at me and said, 'How have you been feeling since
the abortion?'

She had hit a raw nerve and the tears began to flow.

'I feel terrible. I hate myself and all I can think about is that
I'm fat. Please help me.'

She handed me a box of tissues and waited for me to stop
crying.

'OK,' she said, moving her chair nearer to me. 'Chanelle, I
think you have depression,' she said. 'I don't want you to go on
any tablets for it at the moment because you could get addicted
to them. But you certainly don't need any slimming pills. You
need to put on weight, if anything.'

I sat in silence, taking in what she was saying. Depression? Is
that why I loathed myself so much? I guess it made sense.

'I think what you need is some counselling, from someone
who can really understand what you've been through.'

She gave me some leaflets to take away and I decided to start
seeing an abortion specialist. Almost instantly, I started feeling
better. It really did help to talk to someone neutral about it and
to know I wasn't alone. Unlike the patronising therapy I'd had a
few years ago, this was more adult and I found I could open up
easily. The counsellor I saw never judged me, and said, 'You have
nothing to feel guilty for. What you did was not wrong. You need
to let go of these feelings to allow your body to heal mentally.' It
all made sense. 'Stopping eating is probably a reaction to the
trauma you've been through and a way of taking back control,'
she said. 'But you don't need to punish yourself in that way.'

Over time, I began to come to terms with it all. I started

eating properly again, stopped the crazy workouts and, gradually, felt the self-hatred melt away. At last, I felt I could get on with my life again. All this time, I hadn't heard from Spencer but one day, about six months later, he called me up unexpectedly and said, 'Chanelle, can we meet? It's really important. I need to talk to you.'

'How dare you call me?' I said. 'You have no right to get in touch after what you did to me. I have nothing to say to you.'

'Please, just give me ten minutes to explain some stuff to you,' he persevered. 'Then you never need see me again.'

In the end, I agreed to meet for a brief talk. I didn't want to open up old wounds but I suppose I was also curious. I'd never got any answers about why he behaved like he did, so this could be the final piece in my closure.

We went for a drive and, after a few awkward minutes, I pulled over the car.

'Do you realise how much you hurt me?' I started off. 'Don't think anything you can say will ever take that away. Because it won't. The way you abandoned me was despicable, Spencer.'

Right then, he put his head in his hands and cried. I'd never seen him do this, so it was quite a shock.

Through his tears, he said, 'I'm so, so sorry. I can hardly live with myself for what I did to you. I hate myself for it. Can you ever forgive me?'

I felt surprisingly calm. It was all done and dusted as far as I was concerned and I didn't want him back in my life.

'Spencer, you broke my heart into a million pieces but I've dealt with it now. It's in the past.'

I'd got the apology I'd wanted at long last, so I couldn't feel angry any more. After having his baby growing inside me for several weeks, I suppose there was a weird bond underneath all the pain.

He looked into my eyes and said, 'So is there no chance we could ever get back together?'

'I've moved on, Spencer, it's too late,' I said. 'I've had to change as a person since what happened. I can't go back now.'

'Please, Chanelle. I know we can get back on track,' he begged. 'Remember how good we were together.'

'Spencer, if I'm honest with you, a part of me will always hate you for what you did. So I can't love you again.'

He nodded sadly and that was that. Who knows, it could have been so different. I occasionally find myself thinking about what we might have had together if he'd been man enough just to admit he had been terrified. But it wasn't to be. He texted me on New Year's Day that year because that's when our baby would have been due. 'Thinking of you today,' he wrote. It was too late for all of that though.

A few months later, shortly before my *Big Brother* experience began, he got back in touch again. 'Look, I'm really sorry, please can you forgive me?' he said, yet again.

'I can't, Spencer. I'm willing to try and look past it and be friends. But I'd never trust you again. I can't picture a future with you.'

But when the calls kept coming, I stopped answering them and told Mum to say I was out if he dropped by. Part of me wanted to try to look past all that hurt but I'd put up a wall that I couldn't knock down.

The next time my path crossed with Spencer's, it was over a ridiculous story he sold about me while I was in *Big Brother*. I'll tell you about that incident later but, in the meantime, there was the small matter of me actually getting into TV's most famous madhouse.

CHAPTER SIXTEEN

This is Davina!

Despite what you might think, it was never my intention to be on *Big Brother*. It hadn't ever crossed my mind. I had this vision of finishing college, going to university and then getting a career as a speech therapist going. So when my college friend Lisa asked me to keep her company while she went to a *BB* audition in Manchester, I agreed but I had no intention of giving it a go myself.

While we were queuing with all the other oddballs, the Channel 4 researchers chatted to the wannabe housemates, homing in on anyone quirky-looking or ultra-loud. After a while, when my feet were beginning to ache, a young guy with a clipboard approached me and Lisa.

'So why do you want to be on *Big Brother*?' he said, looking straight at me.

'Oh, I'm not auditioning,' I told him, putting my hand on Lisa's arm. 'I'm just here to support my friend.'

'Ah, I see. But I'm afraid you can't go any further in the line unless you audition too,' he said with a smile.

I have no idea if that was true or if he just saw some sort of potential in me but, before I could reply, Lisa said, 'Oh, yeah, that's fine. She'd love to audition as well, wouldn't you, Chanelle?'

'Erm, OK. I guess so,' I said, shrugging my shoulders. 'I might as well now we've come all this way.'

And suddenly, the idea didn't seem so ridiculous after all. What did I have to lose – apart from a few hours of my time? It turned out to be quite fun and the interview was straightforward enough – I just had to blather on about myself, which – trust me – is no challenge. Whenever I'm nervous, I speak at a million miles an hour, so I was just gabbling on about anything and everything. I'm surprised they could understand a single word I was saying but it must have worked because, at the end of it, I was asked to fill out loads of forms and someone then called to ask me back for a second phase of interviews. While this was quite exciting, I did feel bad because Lisa didn't get any further and, of course, was disappointed.

'What did you do that I didn't?' she asked.

'I honestly haven't got the faintest idea.' All I can think is that they thought my likeness to a certain Spice Girl was a good selling point because they kept asking me about her. I also told them the story about my real mum's murder and they seemed to think that was fascinating. I guess it helped that I wasn't just some clueless bimbo. In fact, when they did IQ tests on all the potential housemates at the audition, mine came out as 114. This may not actually mean much to you but the average British IQ is 100, so I clearly had more brains than some of the typical airheads in that room!

I was called back a second and third time and, even though I never actually thought I'd get chosen, I went along with it out of curiosity. The whole process was so cloak-and-dagger that it was

This is the only photo I have of me with my real mum Andrea, taken shortly before
he was brutally murdered. Everyone says I look a lot like her.

Above: Joan and Reg were the couple who fostered me after my real mum was killed. They were the most wonderful people and I adored them.

Below left: I think I was a pretty cute baby – even if I do say so myself!

Below right: I loved nothing more than getting stuck into mum's mixing bowls. No wonder I set up my own cake business later in life!

Above: I love this photo of me with my mum Christine – it shows how close we've always been.

Below: Here's my mum and dad when they very young. They've always made such a sweet couple!

Above: I loved my nana Annie, who was my real mum Andrea's mother, but sadly I didn't have the chance to know her very long before she died.

Below left: Enjoying myself as a teenager with my lifelong friend Zoe. She's been a real rock to me through everything.

Below right: When my mum and dad adopted my brother David, our little family was complete.

Above: Here I am with my cute younger brother David. He was adopted too, and we've always been very close.

Below left: This is my first dog, Crumpet the Pomeranian, celebrating my 21st with me. He was later followed by my adorable Chihuahua, Marmite.

Below right: The new Posh and Becks? Ziggy and I were pretty good together before he stitched me up.

Above left: The cover of my pop single *I Want It*. The song actually did quite well in dance charts around the world.

Above right: I was only 6st 12lb in this pic… and miserable.

© *Rex Features*

Below: My party mate Chantelle and I were very close for a while after I came out of *Big Brother*.

Above: I don't look too bad after having just given birth to Blakely! With us are my mum and dad, Christine and Harry, my brother David and Blakely's father, Matthew Bates.

Below: My mum and dad just worship the ground Blakely walks on - but they spoil him rotten!

Above left: Jack and I have had our ups and downs but he's proved that he's a brilliant dad to Blakely.

Above right: A selfie with Jack. Well, why not?

Below: Jack and I took Blakely to Tunisia in summer 2013 - and he absolutely loved it. He wants to live in a hotel now.

quite exciting. One time, I had to get a train from Wakefield to London and was cryptically told to meet a girl with a spotty umbrella at Covent Garden tube station. You'd think I was trying to get into the MI5, not a bloody reality-TV show!

Then, a few weeks before the series began in May 2007, I was called to another meeting where one of the producers said, 'Right, Chanelle, you've made it onto our final shortlist.'

'What? That's amazing,' I said, although I didn't have the foggiest why. 'What does that mean then?'

'Basically, it means that we think you've got the full package,' said this woman. 'You're glamorous, confident and you're clever. Plus you look like one of the most famous celebrities in the world.'

'Thanks very much!' I said.

'So this is where it gets serious. We've selected a number of potential housemates for the final list but, if you want to make the final line-up, you've got to keep it a secret from everyone you know.'

'OK,' I said. 'So I can't tell anyone at all?'

'Well, you'll probably have to let your parents know. But they must be sworn to secrecy too. If this leaks out anywhere in the media, you will automatically be dropped from the shortlist.'

'Right,' I said. 'Don't worry, I'm good at keeping secrets.' Bloody hell, this was intense. But she hadn't finished yet.

'You'll also need to go into hiding for a while, so your identity doesn't leak out.'

'What, I have to live in a cave or something?'

The producer laughed. 'Not exactly but, if you're still keen to be involved, you'll go abroad with a chaperone and keep a low profile for a few weeks.'

'What about college?'

'You'll have to arrange a significant amount of time off. We realise it's a big ask and you might decide it's all too much –

which we'd entirely understand. It's entirely up to you, of course. Perhaps you need to go away and have a good think about it?'

Well, what could I say? 'Oh, actually, I'm going to turn down this once-in-a-lifetime opportunity because I don't want to skip a few lessons or go on holiday for a bit.' As bloody if! Wild horses would not stop me doing this now.

'No, that's all fine,' I said with a nod. 'No problem.'

When I got home, I told Mum straight away. I thought she would kill me for even considering taking off so much time halfway through my A Levels but I was wrong – she was thrilled!

'You're kidding?' she said as I broke the news. 'I knew you were up to something. This is so exciting!' She paused. 'Right, we need to get you some new pyjamas. And you'll need to get your hair done.'

'All right, Mum, calm down!' I said and laughed. 'I haven't got a place yet – there's still a long way to go. But promise me you won't tell Dad. He'll go mad and there's no point until we know for sure whether I've made it.'

'Yes, he will be furious,' she agreed. 'But you can go back and finish your A Levels afterwards, can't you?'

'Definitely,' I said. 'I've worked so bloody hard for them, I'm not giving them up now.'

Mum and I managed to keep our secret from Dad, although it was hard because we wanted to talk about it all the time. A few weeks before the show was due to start, I headed to France with my allocated chaperone, who was called Jenny. Fortunately, we got on really well and we're still friends now. But we had to keep moving around every three days or so, as the producers were so worried about the housemates' identities being leaked. It was completely ridiculous and over the top – I felt like I was in a James Bond film!

It was also a nightmare getting my various different stories straight. I'd told college and my friends there that I needed a few weeks off for an operation on my polycystic ovaries, which they obviously had no choice but to accept. But I'd told my very closest friends that I was going to Cuba for a family wedding because I knew they'd want to come and see me in hospital otherwise! As for Dad, Mum and I cooked up this elaborate fib that I was going on a lengthy field trip to Wales with college. I was leading a total double life!

A few days before the start of the show, Jenny and I came back to London and stayed at the Danubius Hotel, opposite Lord's Cricket Ground in London. I thought by this point that I probably hadn't made it into the final line-up because we hadn't heard anything. I wasn't allowed to go outside at all, so it was quite a claustrophobic experience. Then, the day before the launch, Jenny took the all-important phone call.

'Right,' I heard her say. 'That's great news. I'll tell her.'

As she came off the phone, I grabbed her with both hands. 'What? Am I in?'

'Yes, Chanelle,' she said and beamed. 'You're in!'

Even then, I didn't believe it. 'But maybe they're just saying that and I'm not really,' I said, pacing around the room.

'No, trust me. This is it,' Jenny assured me. 'You are definitely a housemate. A hundred per cent.'

'OH. MY. GOD!' I screamed and we both started jumping up and down. This was the best news ever!

'Let's order champagne,' I said, gasping. 'We have got to celebrate!'

And so we did, late into that night – although Jenny, being the ultimate pro, was careful that we didn't draw any attention to ourselves. It'd be the biggest disaster now if anything scuppered my chances of going into that house.

Although it was still meant to be top secret, I called Mum,

who was beside herself with excitement. 'Shall I tell your Dad now?' she asked.

'No, Mum, we can't! Not when we've come this far. He might phone them up and tell them I can't go in, or go to the press or something. We have got to keep it quiet until I'm in there,' I told her. 'Promise me you won't say anything.'

She, of course, agreed. We both hated keeping such a big secret from him but we knew how he'd react. As it happened, the press had already been lurking around outside our house for several days by this point. God knows how they'd got wind of my name but Dad had been saying to Mum, 'It's strange, the street's very busy today. Why are there so many people out there?'

She'd managed to throw him off the scent and it wasn't until the morning the show began, on 30 May, that he found out the news. A photographer had plucked up the courage to approach him outside our house and said, 'Is it true that your daughter is going into *Big Brother?*'

The penny dropped and Dad stormed inside. 'Christine!' he yelled. 'What the hell is going on? Is it true about Chanelle going on that awful TV show?'

Poor Mum had no choice but to admit the truth and, just as we'd feared, he was so angry he actually phoned up the channel, demanding to speak to the producers responsible. He ordered them, 'Don't you dare put my daughter on TV!'

But because I was 19 and an adult who could make my own choices, they told him the final decision was down to me. And hell would have frozen over before I gave up this golden opportunity. No wonder then that dad actually threw his shoes at the TV when he saw me go into the house that night! Still, it's worth mentioning that his anger didn't last too long because, once the show was underway and all these reporters were knocking on the door offering him £5,000 for an interview, he was like, 'Oh, come on, Christine, let's cheer up! Perhaps it's time to get that new car and some new carpets now?'

Back at the hotel, on launch morning, we woke early and I had to get into disguise for the journey over to the *BB* studios at Elstree. Jenny draped a huge towel over my head and we dashed outside to a waiting car. When we got there, we spent the whole day in a poky dressing room with no contact with the outside world. Not even the production staff were allowed to see me. It was horrible and my nerves were shot to pieces. I felt like crying all day and poor Jenny spent the entire time trying to calm me down. Food was brought to the room on trays as if I was a high-risk prisoner and, if I needed the toilet, I actually had to book in a slot so that I didn't cross paths with any of the other housemates going in and out of their own dressing rooms. It was just insane.

When early evening came, I changed into the Victoria Beckham-style grey dress I'd so carefully chosen and had my make-up done. By now, there were just a couple of hours to go until launch. Jenny gave me a couple of shots of vodka to try and relax me but I kept feeling like I couldn't breathe properly. Eventually, after what felt like the longest wait in the entire world, I was ushered into a blacked-out car and driven the short distance across the compound for my big red-carpet arrival. It was then that I heard Davina's booming voice introduce me: the *BB* adventure was finally beginning.

Once I had escaped the booing crowd and disappeared inside the house, I felt strangely OK. Everyone else there was in exactly the same boat as me, not knowing a soul. I made a beeline straight for the twins, Sam and Amanda Marchant – who you might remember as Samanda. They were lovely and we got on well from the start. But what was weird about the first couple of days is that, out of the 11 of us, there were no blokes at all. So there were a lot of hormones raging, as you can imagine. I actually went into the Diary Room and said, 'Why are there only girls?'

But on the third day, there was a new arrival. An actual guy! For all of us younger ones, this was an exciting development. We needed a man to flirt with and to get the banter going.

It just so happened that the bloke they had chosen to send in was quite hot. His name was Ziggy. And he was about to make my time in *Big Brother* very, very interesting.

CHAPTER SEVENTEEN

The Becks Effect

Ziggy wasn't his real name, of course. He was actually called Zach Lichman and he was a 26-year-old music promoter. He'd also once been a model and in a minor boy-band called Northern Line. They had about three singles before they split up.

He came into the house wearing a smart black suit, white shirt and skinny tie and I couldn't hide my reaction – he was fit! I've watched the clip back on YouTube and my face was hilarious – my jaw was literally hanging open in disbelief and I was jumping up and down on the couch! In her voiceover during his entrance, Davina had said, 'I'm seeing a bit of Posh and Becks happening in the house with Chanelle.' That was clearly what the producers were hoping for too – it was hardly rocket science, was it? To be honest, because I'm an outrageous flirt, I'd probably have been interested in anyone they sent in who was semi-good looking. But looking back, I can't believe I fancied him because now he looks more like a mixture of Cliff Richard and Pat Sharp to me than a demi-god like Becks!

Still, I can't deny the strong attraction between us at the time.

We may have ended up fighting like cat and dog eventually but I genuinely don't think I could have survived being on that show without having him in there.

When he first arrived, all of us girls had been forced to give our suitcases back to *Big Brother*, so we barely had any clothes. But Ziggy gave me one of his grey T-shirts to wear, which I took as a sign that he quite liked me. Then, in his first task, he had to 'date' each of us, one by one, over dinner in a private room. I was the last date and, though it was kind of awkward, there was definite chemistry there. As he somehow ploughed through his 11th course, he told me, 'I think you're lovely. I'm drawn to you.' I was quite taken aback by this. And then he said, 'I've had a lot of dates today but this was one that I've been looking forward to.' That was obviously music to my ears, although it was so weird to be having this intimate exchange so publicly on TV. And I was so nervous that I went and ruined it by blabbing, 'Shall we go to bed?' What an utter idiot.

He looked very confused and spluttered, 'Go to bed? What did you say?'

I tried to correct myself but I could feel my face going bright red. 'I just mean go to the bedroom or into the living room.' Smooth, Chanelle. Really smooth!

Thankfully, the misunderstanding was quickly forgotten and we did end up cuddling up in bed that night. We also shared our first kiss sometime in the small hours and I remember thinking, 'I hope my parents don't see this!'

Things quickly progressed after that and our days were spent chilling out by the pool in the garden together, or lying around chatting in bed. It's surprising how fast we became a proper couple but everything is so full-on in there and magnified about a hundred times, mainly because it is so bloody boring.

In the first few weeks, I felt safe with him; like he was looking after me and protecting me from all the bitching that was going on – mainly at the hands of Charley Uchea. Remember her? She was the one who fancied herself as a real gangster girl and friend of the stars. She actually introduced herself as a 'south-London "it" girl.' How tragic. Ziggy said she was jealous of me but I think she was just an unhappy person inside. During one of our rows, the other housemates had to keep us apart as she screamed at me, 'Posh Spice – you fucking wish! Ugly bitch!' Urgh. She still sets my teeth on edge, even now – but where is she nowadays?

Secretly, I think Charley hated the fact that Ziggy fancied me, not her, so I was more than happy to flaunt our relationship in her face. But, despite what people might have thought, ours was never a 'showmance'. Well, certainly not on my part. I can't speak for Ziggy but I did fall head over heels for him and I remember feeling genuinely elated the moment he told me, 'I love you.'

I didn't say it back to him because it was far too soon for me and, as you know, I tend to be a bit guarded on that whole matter. But to hear him say it was so nice and we were forever making plans for when we got out of the house – from meeting each other's families and friends, to going on holiday together.

We did get physical fairly quickly and it was a frustrating time because we weren't free to act as we would have on the outside world. At first, we tried to keep things under control and, if we slept in the same bed, we'd wear clothes and be inside separate duvet covers. But after a while, we just thought, 'We're adults – we shouldn't care so much about what people think.'

And that's when things did get more heated. Sometimes, I would slap Ziggy's hand away because he was trying to go further but, at other times, I found I was getting caught up in it and it was difficult to stop. Another time, we were in the shower for about an hour and it was getting quite steamy (in more ways than one), so *Big Brother* decided to turn the cold water on! That was a definite passion killer.

So you're probably now wondering exactly how physical we got. And I wouldn't blame you because, when I left *BB*, I saw just how much press coverage we'd generated – it was absolutely crazy. Unbeknown to us at the time, we'd been nicknamed 'Chiggy' and our antics were splashed all over the front pages of the tabloids and celeb mags. And, of course, we'd been labelled the new Posh and Becks. At the heart of all the gossip was the one thing everyone was dying to know: did we actually have sex in there? It's always been a big TV talking point, right from the early days of *Big Brother* 3, when Jade Goody and PJ supposedly got it on under the duvet.

Nobody really seemed to have a clue what had gone on though and, after things had got a little passionate between us one night in bed, Channel 4 decided to release a statement denying that anything too risqué had gone on. They said, 'It hasn't happened. We have looked at the footage in question and it certainly does not look like they were having sex.' Despite this, the bookies still paid out thousands of pounds to punters who had bet on us 'doing it', because so many reports said that we had gone the whole way!

But with it all being a bit inconclusive, it was all anyone wanted to know about when I left the house. Not whether I'd had a fun time or how I was feeling but whether or not I'd slept with Ziggy. Like it was anyone else's business! I remember going on *Big Brother's Little Brother* right after I came out and even Dermot O'Leary asked me outright, 'Did you have sex?'

I looked him dead in the eye and said, 'No. Sorry to disappoint you. No. My mum would have kicked me out of my house.'

And that's the version of events I've always stuck to. I never wanted to look like some cheap, nasty slapper who would go on national TV and do that kind of thing with someone I'd only just met.

But now, all these years later, I guess it's finally time to hold my hands up and tell the truth. I might be at risk of being disowned by my entire family here but, seeing as I'm writing this book in the spirit of total honesty, I can't deny it any longer. So here goes: I was lying. We did have sex in the house. Not only that but we did it every single day for about three weeks!

Without going into too much graphic detail, let's just say we got very good at sneaking off to the bathroom, or disguising it in the bedroom while everyone was asleep. The other housemates didn't have a clue – or at least, if they did, they were very British and didn't say a word about it. Whether the *BB* crew knew or not, I don't know. But they must have because people are watching those camera feeds 24/7. And I did get called in to the Diary Room a few times to be reminded to take my contraceptive pill! Why would they say that if they weren't aware of what we were up to?

It's not something I'm particularly proud of and, if I had my time again, I think I'd be far more restrained – although that's easy to say in hindsight. You might think badly of me but I honestly didn't realise that people would know what we were doing – the bedroom was always pitch-black at night and you forget that there are night-vision cameras and microphones all around you. That sounds silly I know but it's true.

I do feel bad that I lied about it but I've always been afraid of being judged and, let's face it, while Ziggy would probably have got a big slap on the back for it, I'd be the one branded a slag. Totally unfair, of course, but that seems to be the way things work in our hypocritical society. But while I used to be terrified about what people might think of me, I don't really care any more. I was 19 and having a once-in-a-lifetime experience that most people will never have. And it's not like it was some sordid one-night stand – we were a couple by then; that's what couples do. Besides, what we did on *Big Brother* was pretty tame compared to the outrageous stuff that goes on in *Geordie Shore* nowadays!

But whatever, it's all water under the bridge. And if you watched the show, you'll recall that it wasn't long before things turned sour and we began having blazing rows. It wasn't just idle bickering either – we seemed to bring out the very worst in each other. We argued about everything – I hated him smoking and accused him of having bad breath; another time we had a massive fight over me playing the violin for a task and it kicked off when I started squeezing the other housemates' spots! It was all so petty but the rows got so out of hand. He called me an 'attention-seeking hypochondriac', which really upset me and I began to feel swamped by all the negative feelings.

At least nobody could say we were boring because we broke up and got back together so many times over those weeks that even we lost track! At one point when he broke up with me, he actually used the most cringe-worthy words of all time: 'It's not you, it's me.'

I sat there aghast and said, 'Oh my God. You just used the words "it's not you, it's me" on national TV. How embarrassing is that?' And it really was mortifying. What an idiot.

Eventually, the rows became too much to bear. I really do think I was having a mental breakdown in there and I demanded to leave. The producers must have been concerned over my state of mind because they let me out and sent me straight to see a psychologist. Once I'd calmed down, they tried to convince me to stay. And to cheer me up, they said, 'What do you think Victoria Beckham would do in this situation?'

I snapped, 'How do I know? She's in bloody America!'

Although I did eventually agree to go back into the house, it was only temporary, as the fights with Ziggy flared again almost instantly. It all came to a head during one massive final row, when I knew I had to get out of there for the sake of my sanity. This time, it was sparked when I accused Ziggy of using my pink towel. Of all the things in the world to squabble about. He started laughing, which was like waving a red flag at a bull.

'You think it's fucking funny, Zach?' I yelled. 'You're acting like a fourteen-year-old child.'

Then he got very angry and shouted at me, 'Who the hell do you think you are? You are so rude.'

I screamed back at him, using the worst language I could find, and then two things finished me off. Firstly, he accused me of being 'the new Charley' and then he accidentally called me 'Sarah' – the name of his ex-girlfriend!

That was it and I let out the loudest, most blood-curdling scream imaginable, right there in the living room. Seriously, I was that rattled. I knew then that my time in *Big Brother* was over for good and I went to the Diary Room, demanding to leave right away.

'I can't live in the same house as Zach,' I sobbed. This time, nobody tried to talk me out of going. So on day sixty-two, after surviving almost nine weeks, I left through the Diary Room door and didn't even say goodbye to anyone.

Although I got so close to the end, I never regretted walking out because there comes a point when you know you've hit your limit. I didn't like the deranged person I was turning into – and I still can't watch back any of the old footage because I find it too upsetting.

To viewers, it might look like some extended holiday in a theme park on TV but the truth is *Big Brother* is mentally challenging and it exposes all of your insecurities and paranoia to the core. You can't truly know how much it screws with your head until you've experienced it first-hand.

And after what I experienced, I really wouldn't wish that on anyone.

CHAPTER EIGHTEEN

Big Brother Fallout

The hours after I left the house were a blur. I was taken to a hotel near the studios in Elstree and had to see a psychologist again, who probably just needed to check I wasn't about to top myself. All I wanted was to get home, back to my own tiny bedroom, and I kept crying and begging to see Mum and Dad.

'They're on their way,' I was told. 'They'll be here soon.'

It was a hot summer's day and I waited in the grounds of the hotel for what seemed like an eternity for them to arrive. Then suddenly, I looked up and saw them walking hurriedly across the grass towards me. I've never felt so relieved in all my life. It was such a corny moment – I ran into their arms and Mum and I were both sobbing, and even Dad looked teary-eyed.

'We're so proud of you,' he said.

'Really?' I gulped. 'But I completely lost it in there. I thought you'd hate me.'

'It doesn't matter, Chanelle. You're out now and that's the main thing,' said Mum.

I instantly felt a million times better with them being there and, from that moment on, my life became insane. That same day, I had to choose an agent and picked PR firm Neon Management, headed up by a guy called Dave Read. He was famous for turning Jordan into a hugely successful and very rich star, so I figured I couldn't go wrong! It was all so alien to me though; I hadn't planned or expected anything to happen after the show and thought I'd just be going home to Wakefield, back to college and to my humble little life.

But 10 minutes after I signed up with Dave, he took a phone call and then said, 'Right, that's your first deal done and dusted.'

'What do you mean? What have I got to do?' I said, baffled.

'Oh, nothing much. You just need to do an interview and have your photo taken by the *Daily Star* newspaper and a couple of magazines like *OK!*, *new!* and *Star*.'

'Right,' I said. 'That sounds good. How much do you think I might get paid?'

Hand on heart, I thought Dave was going to say something like £10,000. And that would have been absolutely fantastic. All I hoped for was a tiny bit of money to see me through the rest of college and to put towards university, so I wouldn't have to live in grotty student accommodation. But what he said next almost gave me a cardiac arrest.

'The deal is for £250,000, Chanelle.'

My mouth fell open. I couldn't speak but Mum was sitting next to me and said, 'What? You're not being serious?'

'I'm deadly serious,' said Dave. 'Welcome to your new life.'

I found my tongue and stammered, 'But why are they interested in me? I just behaved like a total dickhead on national TV.'

'No, Chanelle, you've got something that nobody else has. And after Ziggy comes out of the house, there will be another deal on the table for your first joint interview and shoot. You could both go far with this.'

It was utterly bonkers – especially as, at that point, Ziggy and I weren't even on speaking terms. I'd left the house screaming bloody murder at him and, as far as I knew, he loathed me.

Later that day, in a bit of a daze, Mum and I went to Harvey Nichols in Knightsbridge for some serious retail therapy. I spent about £1,200 on Mac make-up, bought loads of Rock & Republic jeans and got Mum some nice clothes, as well as new jeans for my brother and an outfit for Dad. He tends to wear the same thing every day – one of his blue checked shirts with dark-blue jeans and brown shoes, so I got him a whole new set. It was crazy – we splashed about £5,000 in an hour. We'd only ever been able to window shop in Harvey Nics, so this was a dream come true.

I also needed to work out where I was going to live now I was out of the house because, if there was going to be all this work in London, there was no way I could commute from home every day. I'd been for drinks at the Sanderson Hotel a couple of times before and in that era it was the coolest place to hang out in London. You never knew who you might see sipping a cocktail at its famed Long Bar – everyone from Colin Farrell to Mariah Carey and Paris Hilton were hotel regulars. I had no idea about where to live in London and didn't want to commit to a long rental period somewhere, so I moved into a suite there. I actually ended up staying about four months, which should have cost me about £50,000, but they gave me such a good deal that I only paid about £20,000 in total. It was incredible. My suite had two king-size beds and a separate living and dining area, as well as a huge bathroom kitted out with double sinks and a walk-in shower. I loved it there and the staff made such a fuss of me. They'd give me spare rooms for Mum and my friends and order me in pizza if I didn't want anything off the menu. One day I was walking out of the lobby and saw Usher casually sitting there in a pair of flip-flops. Bounding over like an excited puppy, I shrieked, 'Oh, hi, Usher! How are you?' and he was like, 'Er, hello,' clearly a bit perplexed by this weird girl jabbering away in a Yorkshire accent.

A couple of days after the initial excitement of leaving the *BB* house, Dave sensed a great PR stunt and flew me to LA to go hot on the trail of Victoria Beckham. She was now based there with David and their kids and, though it was basically a glorified photo opportunity, the tabloids loved it. I was taken to all the key Hollywood sites and to an LA Galaxy football match, where David had just started playing. Ironically, he got his first home goal for the club that day and the *Daily Star* ran with the headline: BECKHAM SCORES WITH CHANELLE! Not something I ever imagined I'd read.

Sadly, I didn't manage to hook up with Posh – I guess she might have been a bit busy! The trip was good fun but it was marred by the fact that I kept having anxiety attacks. Some days I didn't even want to leave my hotel room. I guess it was because a lot was being thrown at me and, after seven weeks cooped up in *Big Brother*, all this newfound attention was hard to handle.

I returned home a few days later to a whirlwind of media appearances and photo-calls and suddenly all these lads' mags were desperate to put me on their front covers. I think the first deal I signed with *Nuts* was for £75,000. It was mind blowing.

As the *Big Brother* final approached, I was asked to go back in for a secret task with Ziggy. Although I would never have agreed to return as a proper housemate, I was curious to test the water with him. So with a new hairdo (blonde crop à la VB, of course) and dressed to the nines in a strapless gold dress, I re-entered the house on day 89. Wearing a blindfold, Ziggy had to identify this 'mystery guest' by touch alone and he guessed straight away it was me. But when he took the mask off, he looked like he'd been winded and neither of us knew what to say or do. It was so uncomfortable. After a couple of seconds, we hugged and he told me I looked sensational. So perhaps he did still like me.

'So, is it worth us talking on the outside?' he asked.

'If you want to,' I said. 'I've missed you.' And despite everything, I really had.

As we hugged again, I was told it was time to leave. 'See you on Friday,' he said, blowing me a kiss up the stairs.

At the final, lovely Brian Belo was crowned the winner, and rightly so. He's such a genuine and sweet guy and was more than deserving of his victory. Still, everyone's eyes seemed to be on Ziggy and me and it felt like the whole nation was waiting to see if we'd leap into each other's arms again. As it turned out, he didn't come near me all evening. It was as though I didn't exist. His sister Zoe, who really hated me, was at the party afterwards and she was giving me evil looks all night. So I decided to leave after a bit and go back to my suite at the Sanderson.

He did, at least, call me the next morning to say he'd appointed an agent called Darren Lyons, more commonly known as Mr Paparazzi. Then he said, 'I'm really sorry we didn't get a chance to speak at the party and if I seemed a bit moody. But we've got a shoot with OK! magazine tomorrow, so I'll see you there.'

We basically got paid £125,000 each to dress us up as Victoria and David Beckham and the magazine put us on gold thrones, with me wearing a wedding dress and Ziggy in a white suit. The headline they used was: CHANELLE AND ZIGGY'S POSH WEDDING! We were even asked how long it would be until we knocked up a 'baby Chiggy'. We started at 7am and went right through to about 10pm but it was such an odd day. In front of the cameras, Ziggy was kissing and cuddling me but, as soon as they stopped, he went into another room and didn't want to talk to me. I was so upset; I didn't understand what was going on or why he was being like this. I went back to the Sanderson knackered and confused and the next day I had my own individual shoot, so we didn't speak.

But the day after that, he called me and his attitude had changed completely. He was being so nice and said, 'I'm so sorry. My sister told me you'd been doing bad press about me and screwed me over. I hadn't had a chance to read anything so I was being wary. But now I know you haven't said anything bad and I really am sorry. I do want to see you.'

I did understand where he was coming from because being in *Big Brother* makes you paranoid and you think everyone is out to use you and make a quick buck from you. So we agreed to forget about it and make a fresh start.

'My friend's got a hotel in Bayswater. Do you want to come and stay with me for a couple of weeks?' he said.

'OK, why not?' I said.

I was quite lonely on my own and at that stage I really did want to give things a go with him, so I got a bag of stuff together and went over there.

For a while, things were really good. We became a proper couple and went out for lots of lovely dinners and on romantic mini-breaks. *OK!* magazine also took us to Dubai for another £100,000 shoot but that was a disaster, as I had food poisoning and was horribly sick for the whole five days we were there. I actually panicked that I was pregnant and so took a test – which, thankfully, was negative. There were loads of stories that we'd got engaged out there, which was just silly. There was never any talk of that. I was only 19 – far too young to think about getting married.

Another time, I took him to Center Parcs and he came up to see my friends and family a lot. Although we did argue and had big scenes just like we'd had in *Big Brother*, we regularly told each other we loved each other and it was definitely not a sham. Not on my part anyway.

After a few months, I started renting a plush apartment in Maida Vale, which cost me £4,500 per month, even though it was tiny. If you did a 360-degree turn in the kitchen, you could touch every appliance! But I loved it. The fixtures and fittings were gorgeous and it had beautiful high ceilings and a massive bedroom.

Ziggy moved in with me for a bit but it was around that time that our arguments really started escalating. The biggest problem was that we both got really jealous of each other. We had our own friends and moved in different social circles and, when one would come back from a club really late, the other would automatically be suspicious and start flinging around wild accusations. More of a party animal than me, Ziggy went out almost every night and, of course, girls were throwing themselves at him wherever he went. I lost count of the number of screaming rows we had at 3am. Our poor neighbours.

I guess the fiery side of our relationship did spill over into the bedroom. Our sex life was pretty full on and passionate, which made things exciting, but I didn't think there was anything unusual in that at all – and I still don't.

We kept our rows behind closed doors though and we worked hard to maintain our image as a couple because that's what people seemed to want. We'd learned the rules of the media quickly and I can't deny that the relationship did wonders for my career.

Having said all of that, there were genuine feelings there and Mum and Dad always welcomed him with open arms. It wasn't quite the same story with his family though – they seemed to look down on me and I don't think they thought I was good enough for Ziggy. There I was with my broad Yorkshire accent, like I'd popped straight out of *Emmerdale*, and they were living a very different, affluent life down south.

It used to cause a lot of friction between us. One night I went out to a club in Soho and, by pure coincidence, Ziggy was there with his sister Zoe. It was really tense and, as I tried to have a conversation with him, she started shouting, 'What are you doing with her after all that's gone on?' She stormed out of the club and Ziggy went after her – proving to me exactly where his loyalties lay.

Things were very up and down but, that November, everything changed and he broke my heart in the worst way imaginable.

With my birthday approaching, I'd been making plans for a big party back in Wakefield that Saturday night. I'd booked out a bar called Beluga and arranged hotel rooms for my friends and a lovely suite for Ziggy and me. Loads of my family and friends were coming.

But on the Friday, as I was getting ready to go home, Ziggy said, 'Oh, babe, I've got some family stuff to sort out today. I'm going to stay behind.'

A bit disappointed, I said, 'Oh, OK. When will you come up then?'

'I'll follow you up tomorrow,' he said.

'Well, don't be late for my party, will you?'

'Of course not,' he insisted. 'Don't worry – I'll be there.'

Next morning came and, when I hadn't heard anything from him, I tried calling. No reply. I thought it was weird, especially as we hadn't spoken on the Friday night either, which was rare for us. I tried calling and texting him all day long but could never get through and he didn't reply to my texts. Eventually I rang my agent, Dave Read, in a bit of a state.

'Dave, something's going on. Ziggy's not taking my calls and he's ignoring my texts.'

'Calm down, Chanelle, he's probably hungover in bed,' said Dave.

'No, this isn't like him. Something's happened.'

'All right, leave it with me, I'll call you back,' he said.

Deep down, I was thinking that Ziggy had probably got with a girl the night before and was still with her. While hideous enough to imagine, what was really going on was a million times worse.

'It's bad news, Chanelle,' Dave said when he called me back a little while later.

'Oh my God. What is it? Has he cheated on me?'

'No, nothing like that. I've been trying to get hold of your mum and dad at home so they could break this to you but they haven't been answering their phone.'

'Never mind them, Dave. Tell me what the hell's going on.'

'OK, well there's going to be a big story in the *News of the World* tomorrow.'

'What about?'

'You don't come out of it too well,' he said. 'It says you're violent and have been beating Ziggy up and threatening to kill yourself.'

I was speechless at this. I had no words at all.

'And he's broken up with you,' Dave was saying. 'So he won't be coming to your party.'

Jesus Christ. Ziggy had stitched me up royally. The newspaper had gone to Dave offering me a right of reply but there was nothing we could do to stop them publishing the story. It defied belief. Ziggy and I had been absolutely fine the last time we saw each other and there was no hint of something like this brewing. What an absolute bastard. In a total panic, I tried calling his agent, a woman called Claire I'd always got on all right with.

'It's Chanelle,' I told her. 'I need to speak to Ziggy urgently. What the hell has he been saying to the *News of the World?*'

But Claire calmly replied, 'Please don't ever call this number again.'

Then she hung up.

It was so frightening. It seemed I had no choice but to wait it out and see what rubbish he'd come up with and, as you'd expect, I had the worst time at my party and felt sick all night. How could I let my hair down when the biggest newspaper in the country was about to print some mystery exposé on me that I had no control over? At midnight I went online on my Blackberry and saw exactly what he had to say about me. It was their front page story and Ziggy's sad face was splashed next to this horrendous account of me being a psychopath who he thought was going to kill him! What the actual hell?

It really was the biggest load of crap I'd ever read in my life. He said that I repeatedly and violently attacked him, leaving him with black eyes and cuts all over his body. 'If we'd stayed together, she could have killed me,' he told the paper.

Not only that but he even said I frequently ordered him to beat me up in bed. He claimed:

> Chanelle loves aggressive sex. Guys have knocked her around in bed but I'm not into that. I walked away from sex sessions battered and bruised.
>
> My back would be ripped to pieces by her scratching. One night we were in the middle of sex and she said, 'Hit me in the face.' I refused. I would never hit any woman, let alone while having sex with her.

I could not take any of it in. It was like he was ripping my heart out of my chest with both hands. And you only have to look at the difference in our sizes to see that was crazy; he's a 6ft, strapping guy and I was a tiny size 8 who weighed less than 8st. As if I could beat him up or make him believe I'd kill him. I'd been to a few boxing classes prior to that and my trainer was in

140

stitches laughing for 10 minutes because I was so pathetically weak and feeble.

Yes, I threw stuff around in the flat when we argued and I did try to shove him in the heat of a row. I also admit I slapped him round the face once or twice – but that doesn't mean I was capable of killing him.

As for things in the bedroom, yes, our sex life was uninhibited but plenty of people are like that. It doesn't make you a psychopathic would-be murderer, does it? I also bruise very easily so, if things had been as aggressive as he said, I'd have been walking around black and blue, wouldn't I?

He also said I'd threatened to take an overdose after we fought but that was just him manipulating the past because he knew about my previous experiences and used it to his advantage. That was so underhand and nasty.

The most laughable bit though was his claim that, if he wanted to talk to me, I'd pass him onto my PA to arrange a time for us to speak. What a load of utter bollocks! I'm from Wakefield, I'm not the Queen – I didn't need anyone to answer my phone. It was permanently glued to my hand in those days.

The next day, all my friends came round to Mum and Dad's for a prearranged champagne breakfast but I just sat against the radiator in the living room, crying inconsolably all day long. Nobody knew what to say.

How could he betray me like this? I was so confused. He was supposed to have cared about me. I knew we had big arguments and I had tantrums but you don't do this sort of thing to someone you've ever had feelings for. Not in a million years. If I'd known he needed cash so badly, I'd have bloody written him out a big cheque myself.

I tried calling him on his mobile but he'd changed his number by this time. And Dave couldn't offer me a shred of comfort.

'I want to sue the paper,' I told him.

'You can't do that, Chanelle. The *News of the World* is the most powerful newspaper in Britain. Do you really think you can afford to take them to court over this? Don't be silly.'

'What am I supposed to do then? I can't believe I've been so vilified – it's completely unfair.'

'You've just got to ride it out,' he said. 'It'll blow over. Tomorrow's fish-and-chip paper and all that.'

As it happened, Dave did arrange for me to tell my side of the story to another newspaper and magazine but what could I really say to stop the damage to my reputation? It had already been done as far as I was concerned.

For the next few days, I was so depressed I couldn't even go out of the house and I lay around in my pyjamas full of despair. Mum and Dad were understandably devastated too, as Ziggy's actions had also heaped shame on them.

Unsurprisingly, I never heard from him after all of that. Not a whisper. And it wasn't until a couple of years later that our paths crossed again. We were both in Marbella with groups of friends and, when I saw him, my stomach lurched – not in a good way. Seeing him brought back such awful memories and, though I had nothing to say to him, he came over to speak to me.

'Hi, stranger,' he said. 'I haven't seen you in a while.'

I felt like it was some sort of piss-take and that I was being filmed for *Punk'd*.

'Oh, hi,' I said, as nonchalantly as I could.

'I just wanted to come over and clear the air,' he said. 'Things got really twisted in that interview and they made out it was much worse than it was. I was really mad about how they made you look.'

I was not in the mood for this. 'Don't bother,' I told him. 'I know you got more than £100,000 for that interview, so of course you had to say certain stuff.'

He looked at me gratefully but I wasn't finished yet.

'If you want to be a man and apologise, fine but don't lie to my face because I'm not stupid.'

He held his hands up and said, 'OK, I know. I'm sorry. I was young and foolish and I was getting bad advice and hanging around with the wrong crowd.'

That fleeting little apology could never undo what he did. Nothing could.

'Well, I'd like to get on with my holiday now,' I said, walking away. 'See you later.'

I just couldn't be bothered to waste my evening talking to a drip like that all night. And he still hadn't cut his ridiculous hair!

You might imagine that was the last I ever heard from him but, some time later, I got a text from him, which said, 'Hi, it's Zach 'Ziggy' Lichman.' Like I'd ever forget that name.

'I was just saying hi, I wanted to see how you were,' he wrote. 'You're looking amazing at the moment.'

I could only assume that his money had dried up and he was trying his luck.

'Your career's going really well too, isn't it?'

'Yeah, things are going well,' I said, trying to make light of it. 'You actually did me a real favour selling that story.'

Then he asked if I was planning any trips to London and if he could take me out for dinner if I came down. Who the hell was he kidding?

'No, I don't really fancy that,' I texted back.

'Oh. Why not?'

'I'm just not interested.'

'Come on, just as friends having a catch-up.'

'But we're not friends, are we?' I said. 'We've got nothing in common.'

His ego was really that big that he thought I might consider seeing him again. The gall of the man was astonishing. In the end, I told him not to contact me again. This was one can of worms I really didn't want to open.

Still, Ziggy wasn't the only guy to 'kiss 'n' tell' on me. While I was in *Big Brother*, my old flame Spencer decided to tell a rather different version of my abortion drama, saying we'd been through a miscarriage together and that he'd loyally held my hand all the while I'd been in hospital.

When I read that, I was like, 'Wow. Just wow.' I confronted him and he said, 'I only did it because I didn't want you to look bad for having an abortion.'

To be fair, part of me understood his logic, as many people have very strong anti-abortion opinions. But to say he was right there with me, dabbing my face with water and stroking my hair as we lost our child, was so insensitive. How could he say all that when he'd put me through hell?

In the interview, he also said that we'd been together when I went into *Big Brother* and that he now wanted to beat Ziggy up. This was the final straw for me and I wrote him a letter, which I posted through his door. It said something like, 'I think what you've done is disgusting. I'm really upset that you've made yourself out to be such a nice person when, in reality, you almost ruined my life. You can't muck about with these issues, especially when someone's life has already been so messed up.'

After he read it, he dashed round to our house. I wasn't there but he told Mum, 'Christine, I'm so sorry – I never meant to put her through that. I was young, I didn't realise what she was dealing with. I just want to do the right thing now.'

In all honesty, I don't think he's a nasty person; he just wasn't ready to be a dad and, in blind panic, tried everything he could to stop the situation going any further. I've seen him a few times since and he's helped me out with a couple of odd jobs at home.

He probably still feels guilty, so I'm sure he'll always help me out in future if I need him. Perhaps I almost sound a bit too forgiving of Spencer but I guess it's easier that way than to hold a life-long grudge. Life's too short for so many enemies, isn't it?

CHAPTER NINETEEN

The Dark Side

The post-*Big Brother* whirlwind continued and a steady stream of work came my way – including loads of raunchy glamour shoots. People have often asked me how I feel about doing them and I often get accused of being a slag for stripping off. But it's a job like any other, isn't it? And it happens to be one that pays very well, so I've never been ashamed of it. If my body helps sell magazines, who is anyone to judge that?

I was obviously a bit nervous about what Mum and Dad would think in the early days, especially about some of the 'girl-on-girl' type pictures, but they're shrewd enough to know why I'm doing it. They've also kept every publication I've ever been in so, if their house ever burns down, about £10,000-worth of magazines will go down with it! And I think Dad genuinely feels proud that his daughter is a model and loves hearing compliments about me – even if it is in relation to me having my boobs out!

In November 2007 I filmed a reality-TV show for VH1 music channel, which was called *Wannabe* (what else?). The presenter,

Toby Anstis, and I had to find a new girl group similar to the Spice Girls and it was a sort of downmarket *X Factor*. But sadly, the band we created failed to achieve quite the level of world domination of Posh and her girls. You win some, you lose some, I guess.

Soon after, I got my beloved dog Crumpet, a ginger Pomeranian who I just adored. She was a little cheer-up present to myself after I had my fingers burned by a footballer called Seb Hines, who played for Middlesbrough.

He'd got my number from a club promoter I knew and, after we'd been out a couple of times, the newspapers cottoned on to it. Nothing had happened between us – we'd only been to the cinema and for a bite to eat but the next minute there was this big story in the *News of the World*, saying he had a kid and a girlfriend who was pregnant with their second child!

What on earth had I got myself caught up in? As far as I was aware, Seb was totally single and he'd never mentioned a child at all.

I called him up in a state and said, 'What the hell is this about? Have you got a girlfriend?'

'Er, yeah but we're in the process of breaking up,' he said lamely.

'Oh Jesus, Seb, this is not on. Please can you tell her that I never knew about this?'

After that, I wanted nothing more to do with him. I'd thought he was a bit of a drip anyway and we didn't have much in common, so I called it all off before it got any messier.

The weekend the story came out, I was at Center Parcs with my friends, Alison and Zoe, and I was so fed up about being portrayed as this trampy girl who broke up people's relationships that they took me off to Manchester to buy Crumpet. She definitely made me feel a lot better – and then, soon after that, she made her TV debut in the second show I did for VH1, called *Wannabe Popstar*. This one followed my bid to release a single called 'I Want It'. Although I am actually a good singer and did really well at GCSE Music, it was so hideously embarrassing and cheesy. Saying that, it got to No.2 in the UK dance chart and the remix went to No. 5 in Russia, so it can't have been that terrible.

I got paid about £75,000 in all to do the song, which included a nationwide tour as well as a music video. And that was the bit I absolutely hated. During filming, they put me in a tiny corset and knickers and bra and I just wanted to cry. But for that kind of money, I could hardly complain, could I? That was my life now: Dave would just tell me what I was doing and I had no say at all. For instance, if Victoria Beckham changed her hair, he'd book me an appointment at a salon and tell me to get exactly the same style. I know I was doing very well out of it but it was like he had power of attorney over my whole life.

So there I was in this video, gyrating all over the place and looking like a right tart. And watching it back, all I could think about was how fat I looked.

'Look at my bum – it's disgusting,' were the first words I said.

Straight afterwards, I went and had liposuction done on six different areas of my body – including bum, thighs, arms and tummy. It was silly really because I was only a slim size 8–10 but I had begun to see myself in a whole new light.

This, I'm afraid, is where I started to experience the real pitfalls of fame. I'd started feeling very body conscious as soon as I'd come out of *Big Brother* and hit the trail of celeb parties and events. Dave had a lot of models on his books, and I was constantly comparing myself when we all went out, thinking I was too chubby next to them.

I remember moaning to one girl about my thighs on a night

out and she said to me, 'Why don't you do coke? It makes you lose so much weight.'

A lot of the girls in the clubs were really into it and would do it in the toilets of places like Chinawhite. I just thought it was a vile and disgusting habit – I'd far rather have a glass of Moët any day!

With a spiralling belief that I was too fat, it was around this time that I'd become good friends with the *Celebrity Big Brother* star Chantelle Houghton, who Dave also represented. She was the one who had gone in as a 'normal housemate' in 2006 but beat all the real celebs to win it. Chantelle married the Ordinary Boys singer Preston soon after meeting him on the show but it all fell apart in a matter of months and she became badly bulimic as a result. She very publicly admitted her issues and told how they'd go to posh restaurants where she'd eat huge bowls of pasta and then have a big dessert, before going home and sticking her fingers down her throat to bring it back up.

Now don't get me wrong, I've always liked Chantelle and we had a brilliant time together a few years back. But I can't deny that her eating disorder had a massive influence on me. I don't blame her for one second – I was a grown adult and responsible for my own actions but it was hard to be around someone so hung-up on food and not get sucked in. After already dealing with mild anorexia following my abortion, I guess I was still susceptible to using food as some kind of control mechanism.

I didn't know many people in London, so Chantelle became a close confidante of mine. But she was still openly bulimic and wouldn't hide it from me at all. She was forever obsessing about what she ate and it made me really start thinking about what I was eating. We went on quite a few holidays together and, if we went out for dinner, she'd go back to our room and straight into the bathroom to make herself sick. She was losing weight so easily and I remember saying, 'God, I feel really fat compared to you. My arms look massive. I hate them.'

One day, I decided to try and make myself sick too. But it's actually harder than you'd think. I tried with my fingers and it didn't work; I tried using a toothbrush – that didn't work either. I even used a chopstick but still nothing happened. I didn't understand how Chantelle could do it so effortlessly. So I went on the Internet and looked at all these pro-anorexia and bulimia sites telling you how to purge yourself. It was very easy to find this information, which is so dangerous for young girls.

I made up some username like 'Skinnydream' and, using the guidance from one of these sites, taught myself how to do it. It was horrible. I really loathed doing it – I hate being sick, even when I'm poorly. And, while Chantelle could look completely normal afterwards, it left my eyes streaming and mascara running down my face and I'd be all sweaty and carry on gagging for ages.

Within a few days of making myself throw up for the first time, I thought, 'This isn't for me. There must be another way.' So instead, I started really cutting down on what I ate and stuck to chicken with vegetables and no carbs. But as I got more and more obsessed, I began to dislike the feeling of having any food in my stomach at all. I invented a concoction made up of a tin of tomatoes and half a chopped pepper, mixed up with some Tabasco sauce and a clove of garlic. Some days that's all I would eat. Occasionally, as a treat, I'd divide up a packet of Hula Hoops into three clear plastic bags and make them last for three days.

On that basis, you'd think I would have quickly started to waste away but the frustrating thing was that I was still going out a few times a week, so getting a fair amount of calories from champagne and cocktails. And if our crowd was going out for dinner, I had to join in and actually eat. But, unlike Chantelle, I just couldn't cope with regurgitating it all later.

That's when I found my answer. I stumbled across some laxatives in my local supermarket and, amazingly, they came in the form of little chocolates, so it seemed like they were an actual treat. I'd put them in a Tupperware box and put them in my handbag and, if I ate one, people just thought I was having a normal chocolate fix. I got hooked on them immediately and, if we went out for dinner, I'd take several that night. The morning after, I'd be doubled over in pain on the toilet and wouldn't be able to get up until the afternoon.

After a while, my cleaner, Jessie, started to grow suspicious. She was from Thailand and just the nicest lady. I always told her not to but she'd go above and beyond her duty, doing all kinds of odd jobs for me. She came in two mornings a week and each time would bring me breakfast in bed.

I'd say, 'Oh, I'm so sorry, Jessie, I really don't want anything. I feel really sick.'

'Is your stomach playing up again?'

'Yeah,' I'd tell her. 'I've got the worst cramps and diarrhoea.'

She eyed me carefully. 'You're always in bed and feeling ill. You should go to the doctor's.'

'I know, I will,' I fibbed.

Bless her, she was so concerned and would shake her head: 'You're not well – this is not normal.'

One morning, she was emptying my bathroom bin and came out holding up several laxative packets.

'What are these?'

'Oh, they're nothing,' I said.

'Have you been taking all of these, Chanelle?'

'No, you really don't need to worry about me.'

'Come on, what's going on? You can tell me.'

I made up some lame excuse that I'd found the laxatives in a cupboard and thrown them away.

'But why are the packets all empty?' she said.

'Oh, I threw the actual tablets down the loo so I'd never be tempted to take them,' I replied.

'Hmm,' she said, obviously well aware I was lying – but what could she do?

Gradually, the weight did start to fall off me and things then took a turn while I was doing one of my weekly shoots for the *Daily Star* with the photographer, Jeany Savage. Lying on the floor for a shot, I suddenly went really dizzy and my head hit the floor. It wasn't like I'd fainted as such but I was really weak and lost control of my body.

'What's the matter with you?' said Jeany.

'I'm so sorry, I'm so hungover,' I bluffed.

'Right, let me make you a bacon sandwich,' she said.

'Oh, no thanks, I feel sick.'

'What about some crumpets then?' Jeany was so funny like that, always trying to feed me up.

Later, she said, 'Have you been dieting, Chanelle? You look so thin at the moment.'

'Really?' I said and grinned. 'Thanks!'

'No, I don't mean it as a compliment. Your ribs look disgusting. I don't think we're going to be able to airbrush them out.'

I just laughed. 'You crack me up, Jeany.'

'But I'm not joking, Chanelle, the *Star* aren't going to like these shots. You're too skinny. You need to put some weight on.'

The week after, Dave came with me on another shoot for the paper. As we were looking through the shots on a computer with Jeany, she said, 'We're going to have to make your boobs look bigger on these. You don't have any any more.'

And it was true: my bra size had dropped down to an AA.

'We'll need to blend your ribs in too.'

But I just wasn't getting it. 'Do you think you can take a bit off my arms too? They look really big.'

Dave butted in and said, 'No way. You've got nothing to lose off your arms, or any of you, for that matter.'

We were basically seeing a completely different photograph – one which I thought I looked massive in, even though I was only about 6½st. I was roughly the same size I'd been when I'd had my eating issues after the abortion but still I wanted to be thinner. My goal was to be 85lbs, which is about 6st.

As I was changing, I heard Jeany tell Dave, 'The paper have seen the untouched pictures and they don't like them. They think Chanelle's too thin. She's going to lose her contract if she doesn't put on at least a stone.'

At that time, I was earning about £3,000 a week from the *Daily Star*, so to lose the contract would have been awful – for Dave as well as me.

'You look horrible,' he told me bluntly. 'You're not going to get any more lads' mag covers unless you put on some weight.'

And he was right – curvier models do always sell better than the really skinny girls. These magazines do like the glamour girls to be womanly and have boobs and a bum. Something to grab hold of, as they say.

I was thrown into a panic by his words but he hadn't finished yet. 'You look ill, you've got bags under your eyes, you've always got stomach ache,' he said. 'It's not professional to be like this on shoots.'

What could I say? I really did look and feel awful – but I still wanted to be slimmer. Living down in London, it wasn't like I was seeing my family or friends that often, so I didn't have anyone to tell me to get a grip and get some proper food down me. I was hanging out with all these models and, because I'm so petite at 5ft 3in, I blended in.

I'm not sure if Dave had any idea I was taking laxatives but I think he knew that Chantelle and I were in a bit of a competition to lose weight. So, from then on, he tried to separate us, assigning her to a different agent and making sure we didn't go to the same events. It didn't stop us texting, calling and meeting up though. She was still probably the only real friend I had down south.

But because I was scared about losing all my contracts, I did cut down on using laxatives, although it was hard because I was still convinced I was fat and hated myself whenever I went out for dinner.

Around this time, a change for the better came about when a mutual friend introduced me to the footballer Danny Simpson, who went out with Tulisa from the X Factor a few years later. At the time, he was playing for Manchester United and was one of the big up-and-coming stars. We started texting a lot and I was quite drawn to him – especially after finding out that he was a real family man and adored his mum so much that he'd bought her a lovely house. He was ambitious too and, as a professional footballer, was more clean living than some of the druggy people I'd been mingling with in London.

Although it was never overly serious, Danny turned out to be a guy I'd see intermittently over the next 18 months and dating him definitely helped me deal with my food issues. Staying up with him in Manchester, we'd go out for dinner a lot – either to a Chinese restaurant, where all the footballers like Wayne Rooney and Rio Ferdinand went, or to Nando's. The crux of it is that I had to eat normally with him. It was a new relationship and I didn't want him to think I was a psychopath. Plus I didn't want to be taking laxatives at his place and spending all day on the toilet! Can you imagine anything more embarrassing? So by default, I kind of snapped out of it altogether. I started going to the gym with him, got my energy back and put on a few pounds.

But because I was working out, I was toned and had muscles. People said I looked better than in ages and I genuinely felt that way too.

I guess, in some ways, I was lucky that I could get better through spending time with Danny and also by not wanting to lose my modelling contracts. Some girls obviously don't have that chance and that's when eating disorders can spiral out of control. I was able to sort out my weight issues because my circumstances meant I needed to.

And while I've been dieting like mad this year after putting on 3st, I've been doing it sensibly and by eating super healthily. If I cut down on carbs as well as alcohol, the pounds do fall off. I think my weight will always fluctuate – as you'll know if you saw some rather unflattering pictures of me in a bikini on the beach in Tenerife in December! But I'm relaxed about it nowadays and I'd definitely never touch laxatives again. I just couldn't go through all that again – I don't have enough time to sit on the toilet all day, for starters!

CHAPTER TWENTY

Back To My Roots

Eventually, life in London began to grind me down and I was more and more homesick for my friends and family back home. My on-off romance with Danny had also fizzled out again after – surprise, surprise – I found out he was messaging other girls, and I was a bit disillusioned by the circles I'd been moving in. It felt like I was losing the 'real' me amidst all the bitching, backstabbing and cheating that went on in showbiz.

I was also sick of the constant pressure to look good and the way that girls would compete to get 'papped'. I realised how crazy it had become when I went to get my lips plumped one day and had the most hideous reaction to the injection. The day after, I was out for dinner at Nobu with Dave and some of the guys and my lips just kept on swelling. In the end, they got so big I looked like Lesley Ash. I had to have antihistamines injected into them to decrease the size but then my tongue swelled up too and I had to cancel all my work for a week. What a joke.

Nowadays I'm much more careful and, though I do still occasionally have my lips done and the odd bit of Botox once a year or so, I only see a specialist that I'd trust with my life. Ultimately, I am happiest in my pyjamas, with my hair scraped back off my face and wearing no make-up.

I began making plans for a quieter life and set about finding my own place to buy in Wakefield. It was a decision made all the easier as I'd also ended up starring in a fake sex tape for MTV that April, which proved to be a massive headache. Let me get this straight: I categorically didn't want to do it and, if you've not seen it, please don't go and Google it! But it all came about when Dave said, 'I've got a great job for you. You're going to do a sex tape with a puppet!'

'What are you talking about?' I said. 'There's no way I'm doing a sex tape, Dave.'

'But it's not real. It's with a puppet. It'll be a laugh.'

'No way, it's not going to happen.'

'It is going to happen – I've signed the contracts,' he said.

'But I've not authorised you to sign any contract, so I'm not doing it.'

'Yes, but you signed a contract authorising me to represent you and to sign deals on your behalf. And that's what I've done. So you are doing it.'

We argued back and forth for days but, despite being offered £15,000 for just two hours' work, I was dead set against it.

'Look,' I persisted. 'I'll pay them £15,000 and they can pay someone else to do it.'

'You're being really silly,' Dave said. 'It's funny. It's a viral advert. Learn how to laugh at yourself – who cares?'

'But I don't want to. It's not funny. My mum and dad will go mad. I can't do it.'

'Come on, it's no different to Leonardo DiCaprio and Kate Winslet having sex in *Titanic*.'

'But they were acting in a film – that's different.'

'Well, think of this as an acting job then. But you're doing it and that's the end of it.'

A few days later, I went along to the shoot, was really pleasant to everyone and got the job done – but I was so angry that I didn't speak to Dave for a week. The clip was shot in semi-darkness and I was rolling around on this bed in my underwear. And then I had to pretend I was having full-on sex with this horrible frog-like puppet wearing sunglasses. The disgusting thing was spanking me and shouting, 'Yessss!' How utterly grotesque!

Up to this point, there were usually just a couple of photographers outside my apartment every day but, after the ad went viral, there were 25 of them out on the pavement. My neighbours were furious with me for causing such chaos but I was like, 'What can I do?'

I can at least laugh about it now but it was the most humiliating thing I've ever done. I was especially mortified as Mum and Dad got abuse on the street over it and their house was egged. I just knew then that I couldn't carry on with that kind of lifestyle. I'd always done everything Dave wanted me to do and, of course, I was very grateful to him for helping me forge such a lucrative career but I was coming up to my 21st birthday and it was time for a change.

I bought my first house in Horbury, near Wakefield that autumn, which was so exciting. It cost about £380,000 and it was my dream home, with six bedrooms across three storeys. I got the whole top floor knocked into one big bedroom and turned two of the other rooms into an office and gym. I was thrilled with the house and, when I got the cutest long-haired Chihuahua called Marmite to keep me and Crumpet company, I had my perfect little family.

It felt so significant to have bought my first place by the time I'd reached 21 – like I was finally a proper, responsible grown-up.

On the day of my birthday, we had a champagne breakfast at Mum's and then about 10 friends and I took the train down to London, where Dave was throwing me a glitzy party at Embassy nightclub. We checked into St Martin's Lane Hotel, all had a relaxing massage and then ate dinner in the hotel restaurant.

The party was great fun and I was glad that my sisters came down, while celebs like Calum Best and Brian Belo also dropped in to wish me a happy birthday.

The night after my party, we all got the train home, hungover and tired, and went back to mine to watch DVDs and cook a big roast.

It was a good time and I loved playing homemaker and finally seeing my post-*Big Brother* earnings come to good use by getting on the property ladder. But my resolve to stay single hit the buffers in February 2009 when I got a text right out of the blue from yet another footballer, this one called Matthew Bates.

'Hi,' the text said. 'How are you?'

'Who's this?' I wrote back.

'I'm Matt Bates. I play with Seb Hines.'

Oh, for God's sake. What were these blokes like?

'What do you want?' I texted back.

'I was just wondering if I could take you out on a date.'

Unamused, I replied, 'What do you think I am, the Middlesbrough-team bike? Don't you feel a bit awkward?'

'Seb said you were just friends.'

'We are.'

'So would you like to go for dinner some time?'

As our text exchange went on for a bit, I started to feel a bit curious, so agreed to meet him. He was a year older than me but, because I'd never even heard of him, I had to Google him to see what he even looked like. I wasn't sure at first because he had a bit of a skinhead in some of the pictures I found but then I discovered that he'd shaved it all off for charity after his friend died, which I thought was really sweet. But on our first date, I think my first words were, 'Thank God you've got hair!'

We went to a nice pub and had steak and mash, which is my favourite meal ever, and it was one of those rare first dates that was easy and natural. I wasn't looking to meet anyone, so there was no expectation on my part but I found I really did like him and we laughed all evening. Amazingly for a footballer, he loved books and reading, which instantly appealed to me. Normally, I am quite awkward and geeky in these situations but there was none of that.

You might wonder if I had a thing for footballers but let me get this straight now: I definitely did not! They all just seemed to be very confident about asking girls out, which worked for me because I'm hopeless at making any first approach. Anyhow, if any footballer ever made a move on me these days, I'd be like, 'Go screw yourself!' I've got no time for them any more.

A few nights after my meal out with Matt, he came over to my house and I cooked spaghetti bolognese for us. Not the most original but it was the only thing I'd mastered then. The next morning, I was going on holiday to Mexico with Chantelle – who I was still good friends with – so I didn't want a late night. After dinner, we watched a bit of TV on the sofa and, though we did kiss, Matt was very gentlemanly and left me to get to bed early, saying politely, 'Thanks very much for having me.'

Next day, Chantelle and I flew to Cancun for a fortnight of sun and sea – but I kept thinking of Matt the whole time I was there. I also ran up a £1,000 phone bill because we were speaking constantly. Incidentally, I also got an interesting call from Danny a few days into the holiday. He'd been chasing me again over the previous few weeks, saying he really wanted to get serious this time. But I was so wary of being hurt that I'd been keeping him at arm's length.

'Don't be with Matt,' he said when he rang. 'Be with me. We can make things work. I'm telling you now I'm going to commit to you a hundred per cent.'

'Danny, it's too late,' I said.

But he wouldn't give up. 'Please rethink this before you come back from holiday. Seriously, that guy Matt is an arsehole.' It was a bit confusing to hear all this but I just knew I couldn't trust him. Danny was always going to be playing the field, whereas Matt had already told me he wanted to settle down.

It wasn't the best holiday, especially as Chantelle had her own drama to deal with. She was seeing the footballer Jermain Defoe at the time and got a call from Dave informing her of an imminent 'kiss 'n' tell' by some girl. We were sharing this gorgeous room overlooking the sea but, when she heard the news, she screamed down the phone at Dave and threw a glass against the wall, which smashed everywhere.

I was talking to Matt at the time and he could hear it all kicking off.

'Why don't you change your flights and come home early?' he said. 'I'm desperate to see you.'

'Yeah, OK. I might do,' I said.

The next day, Chantelle and I both flew back. We said our goodbyes at the airport after we landed and that was the last I saw of her for a very long time.

Back home, my relationship with Matt picked up steam and he booked us a weekend away at a gorgeous hotel, which cost at least £800 per night.

'How can you afford all of this?' I asked as he bought me loads of spa treatments and massages.

'I borrowed some money off my mum,' he said. 'I wanted it to be special.'

What was surprising about Matt in those days is that he wasn't some minted, millionaire footballer, flashing his cash around like there was no tomorrow. I was earning more than him with all my glamour shoots in the beginning, so it was sweet that he tried so hard to impress me. But early that summer, he signed a new contract at Middlesbrough and his salary rocketed. He went from being skint to super-rich overnight.

Another thing I liked about Matt was that he was bright. Everyone thinks footballers are stupid but he could hold a good conversation and was competent at having a debate – essential for someone like me who loves an argument! We'd sit around reading books, go for leisurely walks and cycle rides with Marmite and hit the gym together too. He was such a perfect boyfriend that he even took my parents and Zoe out for dinner just to get to know them better.

I couldn't have asked more of him. I'd fallen madly and deeply in love and the early part of summer 2009 passed by in a blur of happiness, with sun-soaked trips to Ibiza, Dubai and Portgual. But perhaps I should have known that it was too good to be true.

One day after he'd been to training, we were in his car when he said, 'I'm having a lads' night tonight. Do you mind staying at yours?'

I'd been living at Matt's house in Yarm, near Middlesbrough almost permanently over the past few weeks but this was no problem at all.

'Yeah, that's fine,' I said and nodded. 'Just make sure you behave!'

I was only joking of course – I trusted Matt implicitly. So I went back to mine and we didn't speak at all that weekend, which was very unlike us. On the Monday morning, while he was at training, I drove up to his place to clear up – assuming it'd be a bomb site after his boys' night. The kitchen was a real mess and, as I started to wash up some of the dirty plates and cups, I saw two wine glasses with lipstick smudges around the rim. My first thought was, 'That's weird; he never said he was having any girls round.' But at that point I wasn't too worried because, if I'd been having a party, I'd invite guy friends over as well as girls.

I carried on tidying up and that's when my stomach did a huge somersault because lying behind the sofa was a girl's lacy bra. 'Oh God. Oh God,' I thought, my mind racing. So that's what had been going on. I felt so sick, not to mention gutted because this relationship had seemed like the real deal. Only a few nights earlier we'd been talking about our future and our dreams of getting married one day, having kids and opening a restaurant together.

I didn't say anything when Matt got back from training – partly because I wanted to be sure before I accused him of doing the dirty on me. We had dinner with my friend Neil that evening and on the way back I saw Matt's phone flash in the car. We had exactly the same Blackberry, so I picked it up, pretending I thought it was mine.

Scrolling through, I saw that he'd been Facebooking several different girls – all of them second-rate glamour models, who had written stuff like, 'Hi, babe, what you up to?'

He'd replied back, saying things like, 'Nice bum in that pic!'

As I looked in horror at all these tarts in their underwear, I fumed, 'Who the fuck are these girls, Matt?'

'Give me my phone!' he shouted, trying to grab it back while he was driving.

'Who are they?' I yelled even louder.

We were right by a Holiday Inn and he pulled over at the side of the road, protesting his innocence.

'It's nothing!'

'Tell me now!'

'Calm down. Why are you being like this?'

Right then, a surge of anger so immense came over me that I couldn't control it. Sitting in the passenger seat wearing a pair of high-heel spiked boots, I began kicking holes in his dashboard and glove box. I was seriously behaving like a total psycho – but even now, I feel livid remembering it.

'Stop it!' he screamed, trying to hold my legs down to stop me causing any more damage. 'Let me explain!'

'Take me home,' I ordered him. 'Drive me back right now. I don't want to hear from you or see you again. You're an absolute arsehole.'

As he pulled up outside my house, the tears were pouring down my face. 'Don't ever contact me again,' I said. 'I can't believe I trusted you. Danny Simpson warned me but I thought you were different to other footballers. And now it turns out it's you who is the total player.'

He said nothing and stared down at the steering wheel.

As I stormed out of the car, I said, 'You told me you wanted to be in a long-term relationship. Why would you do that if you want to play around? At least be bloody honest about it.'

I went into the house, grabbed some of his stuff and started hurling it at his car. I even dented one of the doors by throwing shoes at it so hard.

Finally, he spoke: 'Please, please let me in. I'm so sorry. I love you. Look, I'll delete Facebook. It doesn't matter to me.'

'You mean you have to delete Facebook to resist the temptation of these slags? Can't you just say no?'

I slammed the front door in his face and, though he kept ringing the bell and pleading for me to let him in, I refused. Eventually, he drove off, leaving me a sobbing wreck. I just could not believe this had happened. Looking for some comfort, I called my parents to tell them what had happened but, unbelievably, they sided with Matt.

'Don't throw this away over a couple of harmless messages, Chanelle,' Dad said. 'It sounds like you're overreacting, as usual.'

Mum agreed. 'Matt's a lovely guy. You'd be mad to walk away over something so trivial.'

I could not believe what I was hearing. It felt like another betrayal.

The next morning, after a sleepless night, there was a knock at my front door. It was a florist delivering roses and champagne from Matt. How original! I was totally unmoved, as you'd expect, but this was only the start of it. Every day for the next fortnight, he arranged for a different present to be delivered to my house. He bought me cooking lessons with Marco Pierre White, a spa day for me and a friend, as well as Swarovski jewellery – and each day there would be a card with the gift, which simply said 'Sorry'.

Speaking to Mum again, she said, 'Don't you think you can let it go now? He's only a young lad and all these gifts show he's trying to make it up to you.'

She just didn't get it. 'No, Mum, all these presents mean nothing because he earns a lot of money.'

'Oh, Chanelle. It was only a few messages. Stop being such bloody hard work.'

We fell out badly then. As I've said before, I adore my parents unconditionally but, at times like this, they just wound me up so badly.

'How can you side with him after what he's done?' I was shaking with anger. 'Thanks a lot for the loyalty.' I hung up, having told them I didn't want to see or talk to them – and that was the last time we spoke for a while.

As stubborn and livid as I was, after those two weeks had passed I did start to feel that maybe I should hear Matt out. I'd been blanking his texts and ignoring all his calls until then but late one evening I phoned him, armed with a speech about how he had to prove he could be trusted if we were to have any future. But he must have answered his phone by accident because all I could hear was some girl talking in the background. That obviously stoked my fury again and, with my mind racing, I lay in bed unable to sleep. As I tossed and turned, something told me to go over to his place and find out for myself what was really going on. So like some crazy woman, I got dressed and drove up to Middlesbrough, about an hour away up the A1. It was about 1am by this point but Matt's car was there and some of the lights were on, so I knew he was in. I rang the bell but nobody answered – then I saw what looked like a woman peering through one of the blinds.

'Got you,' I thought. 'You're obviously not letting me in for a reason.'

How was I going to be able to catch him out though? If I came back the next day, he'd only deny everything and whoever was with him would probably have left. I decided there was only one option: I was going to have to sit there in my car until morning.

Thankfully, it wasn't a cold night, so that's what I did, like some lunatic detective. I dozed for a bit but it was bloody uncomfortable and I was also on high alert in case the girl inside the house came out. I knew he'd be leaving for training at around 8am so, shortly before then, I called him. He picked up this time – but, because I hadn't seen anyone leave overnight, I knew he wasn't alone.

'Who are you with?' I said.

Baffled, he replied, 'What do you mean? I'm on my own.'

'No, Matt. You're not. I saw someone looking out of the blinds last night.'

'What the hell are you talking about? Have you been outside my house all that time?'

'Yes, Matt. And now I know exactly what you're up to.'

'You're being ridiculous. Will you just go away?' he said.

'I can't believe you,' I said. 'I was considering taking you back and actually feeling bad for keeping you in the dark. But it turns out you're still doing exactly the same thing as before. You must really think I'm stupid.'

He sighed. 'Look, I don't want to be with you any more, so leave me alone. Get away from my house and don't come back.'

This was like a dagger through my heart. He'd been buying me presents and begging my forgiveness for two weeks and now he was saying this? It must have been because there was some girl there listening in but, still, those words struck me like a hammer blow.

He hung up on me and I burst into tears. I'd got this so wrong. He didn't want me back at all. How could I have been such a fool? I was convinced he loved me and was desperate to be with me but really he hated my guts.

I drove home, barely able to see the road. And the harder I cried, the more irrational I became. I'd fallen out with my parents over Matt and now he'd turned his back on me too. I felt like nobody gave a toss about me at all. In fact, what was the point of me even being around? I'm afraid to say that, once that thought had entered my mind, it was like an old trigger point was reactivated from deep within me. It seemed quite simple – I actually didn't want to be alive any more. I made up my mind then and there: I was going to put an end to this miserable life, once and for all.

CHAPTER TWENTY-ONE

An Emotional Rollercoaster

It might sound like I talk about taking my own life lightly but it certainly didn't feel like I was being flippant back then. Although I'm much tougher and more resilient these days, in my past I could not handle severe hurt or process such negative emotions. So when Matt snapped my heart in two like that, I just wanted everything to stop. I thought, 'I can't cope with that amount of pain again for years on end.' I didn't have the mental or emotional capacity for it.

After I got home from Matt's early that August morning, I walked to the corner shop and bought two packets of paracetamol and then went to the Co-op down the road and bought another two packs.

The lady who served me said, 'Have you got any ID?'

'I'm sorry, are you joking?'

'You've got to be over sixteen to buy paracetamol.'

It shows how rough I looked – I had no make-up on and hadn't even been to bed that night because I'd been waiting outside Matt's all night.

Suddenly, I recognised the woman on the other till. It was the mum of a girl called Amy who I'd been to school with. I said, 'You know me, don't you? I'm the same age as your Amy.'

She said, 'Yeah, that's fine love. But are you OK?'

'Oh, yeah, I've just got really bad hay fever. It's giving me a bad headache, so I'm going to take some tablets,' I lied through my teeth.

When I got home, I opened a bottle of wine and started slugging it back with the pills. In a daze, I'm not certain how many tablets I swallowed but it was certainly a big handful.

Before I fell unconscious, I sent a text to Zoe, which just said, 'I love you so much and I'm really sorry.' I didn't bother getting in touch with anyone else; I was in that frame of mind where I thought no one would care if I died anyway.

Luckily for me, Zoe dropped everything at work and dashed straight round. She had already been feeling anxious because Matt had called her and said, 'I've had a massive fall-out with Chanelle and she's really upset. Can you go and check on her?'

When she arrived, not long after, she started hammering on my front door but I was out cold by then. She says she could see me through the letterbox on the floor and that she was shouting at me but I didn't stir. I'd also thrown up everywhere and was lying in my own vomit.

She called 999 and, when the ambulance arrived, the paramedics got a spare key from my neighbour Lisa and ran into my house, before rushing me to A&E at Pinderfields Hospital, in Wakefield. As she held my hand in the back of the ambulance, Zoe says I kept slurring, 'I want it to be over.'

Once at hospital, I have hazy recollections of the nurses putting drips in me and trying to take blood samples and one said, 'Listen, if you want us to save you, you need to lie still and let me put this in your arm.'

'I don't want to be saved,' I said, thrashing wildly and trying to push her away.

A few of the staff had to pin me down to insert the drip. It makes me so sad to think of myself in such a state and I can see that my behaviour must seem totally selfish. But anyone who has ever plummeted to the depths of mental despair will probably tell you the same thing: you have no control over those black thoughts.

A little later, as the effects of the paracetamol and alcohol gradually subsided, Zoe came back to my bedside and said, 'Matt's here.'

'Tell him to go away,' I begged her. 'He's the one who caused this. He's ruined my life.'

Zoe nodded. She also knew I wasn't on good terms with Mum and Dad but said, 'Do you want me to call them?'

'No,' I said. 'They'll only be mad with me.'

After Zoe left, I slept for the rest of the day and, when I woke early next morning, was told by a doctor that I could go home.

'Already?' I said. 'Are you sure?'

It then became clear the hospital wanted me out as quickly as possible. 'There are a lot of photographers outside, which isn't fair on the other patients and staff,' the doctor said coldly.

Once I'd signed the forms to check myself out, I was led to a back entrance of the hospital, where a taxi was waiting – thankfully with no paps in sight. Back at my house, there was still sick on the floor and an empty wine bottle and tablets scattered all over the place. I wearily cleaned up then went upstairs to bed. When I got up to my room on the top floor, I jumped right out of my skin. There, lying face down on the bed, fully-clothed and fast asleep, was Matt. I'd forgotten he still had a key, so he'd obviously let himself in and crashed out – very considerately choosing to ignore the mess downstairs.

'What the hell are you doing here?' I said, waking him.

He jumped up, rubbing his eyes. 'We need to talk, don't you think?'

'I don't want to see you. Get your stuff and get out.'

'Well what do you think you were doing? That was such a nasty thing to do, Chanelle.'

'What? How can you say that?'

'If you'd have died, it would have been on my conscience forever.'

I didn't have the energy to even get angry. 'Listen, it's not all about you. I've had a stressful enough time as it is. You made me not want to be alive. How can you stand there and have a go at me?'

'What about us then?'

'Just because I'm in a fragile state doesn't mean I'm going to take you back. I hate you for what you've done.'

'Fine,' he said, pulling on his trainers. 'But you really need to think about this.'

Later that day, my neighbour Lisa came round to tell me that my dog Marmite was fine and playing in her garden. Thank God she'd been around to look after him during all the drama. Becca turned up a bit later and made me fish-finger sandwiches but, as we were eating them, Lisa rushed back in. 'Don't be alarmed,' she said. 'But Marmite's run off.'

I leaped up. 'What? Oh God, where's he gone?'

'I don't know. He was here one minute and then he just vanished.'

I ran out into the street, calling for him at the top of my lungs. That tiny Chihuahua meant everything to me. He even came on photo-shoots with me and was always there for cuddles when I was feeling low.

Lisa's husband had gone out looking for him but came back a

while later empty handed. I was so worried and upset. 'I've lost my boyfriend and now I've lost my dog,' I cried. 'It can't get any worse. Nobody wants to be around me.'

Becca and I were out until 3am with torches looking for him. Eventually, shattered and freezing cold, we gave up and trudged home. And there, sitting on the doorstep, waiting patiently, was my gorgeous little Marmite! He's so tiny but somehow he'd managed to find his way back from wherever he'd wandered off to. I clung to him on the ground, almost smothering him! Seriously, I'd never been so happy to see anything in my life and I thought, 'This is a sign that things are going to be OK.'

The next day, I got a call from Dave Read. After asking how I was, he said, 'Right, well, the *Daily Star* are coming up to see you in the morning for an interview about your suicide attempt.'

I'd been worried about it leaking out to the press, as Zoe told me afterwards she'd heard one of the paramedics tell his colleague in the ambulance, 'You know she's the girl off *Big Brother*? The papers would love this.' And sure enough, the story had appeared in the *Sun* the following day.

'But, Dave, I've only just come out of hospital,' I protested. 'I can't do it. My head's not in the right place.'

'Come on, it's a quick ten grand, so it'll be worth it.'

'Dave, I didn't even want to brush my teeth or comb my hair when I got up this morning. I can hardly get out of bed but you want me to do that?'

'Er, yeah.'

I sighed. Once again, it seemed I had little choice but to go along with it. So a team from the *Daily Star* arrived the next morning, taking my picture and asking me all kinds of probing questions. Although I can talk about it quite openly now, it was so hard at the time, especially as I felt so ashamed. Nowadays, there is less of a taboo about depression and mental-health issues but, back then, I felt weak and stupid. I was also dreading a backlash from my interview – I'd been in the media long enough to know that people would think I was making it all up for attention.

Sure enough, when the piece hit the shelves the next day, I got abusive letters through my letterbox saying things like 'Fame-hungry slag' and 'Faker.' But I knew the truth: this hadn't been any lie. In some ways, the suicide attempt this time around had been much more serious than when I'd done it in my teens. I guess back then it had been more like a cry for attention but, on this occasion, I really couldn't see any future and truly felt I had nothing to live for.

As things calmed down following my hospital scare, I started having weekly counselling sessions at the Priory, in Manchester. I didn't want to check myself in because I knew people would think it was a publicity stunt – plus I didn't really want to spend £5,000 a week to stay there. I'm not into therapy at all and think it's self-indulgent but I went along for about three months and I suppose it did help because they gave me anti-depressants, as well as medication for panic attacks and sleeping tablets. I had to go back every few days though because they wouldn't give me too many pills at once, in case I overdosed.

The counsellor I saw there made me talk about everything that had happened but, in my heart of hearts, I couldn't see how that part of the treatment was helping. Why go somewhere just to talk about yourself? The whole experience really opened my eyes to how little support there is for people with mental illness and depression. You are made to feel a bit like a crazy person and so many people must be suffering on their own without a good support network. It's something I feel really needs to be brought to the surface.

Around this time, I received a lovely message from Danny

Simpson, which was so sweet when I was feeling so miserable. He said, 'I know you've chosen Matt over me and that you're in love with him but I'm there for you and will support you. Come and see me whenever you want.'

A few days later, I went over to his house and just cried my eyes out. He was such a good listener and made me feel a lot better. 'I'm sure you'll get back with Matt and work it out,' he said.

It turns out that Danny's prediction was spot on. Over the next few weeks, Matt bombarded me with apologies. 'I thought I was ready for commitment but I obviously wasn't,' he said. 'But now that I've nearly lost you, I am ready. Let's try again. I'm so sorry I've messed things up.'

I was far from convinced by any of his pleas but the situation had been further complicated by Matt picking up a really serious injury while playing in a match that summer. Over the past few years, he'd had a lot of trouble with his left knee and it was threatening to wreck his career. After the latest injury, a scan showed he had cruciate ligament damage, which was a real disaster.

Despondent about being side-lined from the game he so loved, he begged me, 'I can't deal with this on my own. I really need you.'

'Why can't you get one of your other girlfriends to help you?' I replied sarcastically.

'Look, I love you and I want you back. I know how much you love me too – I really think we can make this work. I'll never let you down again, I promise.'

Matt was having an operation on his knee down in London, so I said I would at least visit him – but only as a friend. 'I don't want to be with you but I will support you,' I told him resolutely. I just felt I couldn't abandon him when he was so very low.

I was down for a shoot while he was recuperating at the Lister Hospital in Chelsea and, while I was out for dinner with my friend Jenny later, he phoned me.

'Can you come and see me?' he said.

'OK then. I'll be there in an hour.'

I turned up in a glam dress and heels, as we'd be been for an early dinner, and one of the first things he said was, 'Have you been dating anyone?'

'No,' I shot back. 'I'm still hurting too much for that.'

We carried on chatting for a bit and, after the initial frostiness thawed, I was surprised how nice it was to see him again. We carried on talking over the next few days and I finally agreed to give things another go. You might think I was mad but I've always strongly believed that people deserve second chances in life, especially because I know I'm far from perfect or easy to live with. I didn't want to end up full of regret for throwing this relationship away because, when it was good, it had made me very happy. And I'd never had any concrete proof that Matt had actually done anything with those other girls, had I?

Still, we both knew it had to be different this time around and he voluntarily quit Facebook and MySpace and stopped going out partying. It took a while for me to trust him again but, because we hadn't lost any of that original spark or connection, we gradually managed to get back on track.

He made more effort than ever before too, booking us a surprise trip to Center Parcs for my birthday because he knew how much I loved it there. He also filled his living room with flowers and gifts for me as part of the same celebration.

At the end of November, Matt was still suffering badly with his knee and Middlesbrough decided to send him off for rehab with one of the world's top specialists in Vermont, New England. He asked me to go with him, offering to pay for my flights, so I jumped at the chance. It was an amazing trip and we got on fantastically well the whole time, with no arguments. We had a gorgeous log cabin and there was loads of thick snow, making it so picturesque and romantic. While Matt had his treatment during the daytime, I'd go to the gym, have spa treatments and cook for us and in the evenings we'd snuggle up by the log fire or go to the cinema in our huge American car.

But midway through our month in Vermont, I began feeling a bit off-colour. I was sleeping a lot and my boobs had got a bit bigger and were sore too and I just didn't feel quite right. Before we'd flown out, I'd had a routine check-up for my polycystic ovaries, with blood and hormone tests, but I had absolutely no reason to suspect anything out of the ordinary.

Then, in mid-December I got a call from out of nowhere on my mobile. It was my GP, who said, 'We've been trying to get hold of you at home.'

'Oh, I'm sorry,' I said. 'I'm in the States. What's the problem?'

'Well, we've got your test results back and they're showing a really high level of HCG, which is a pregnancy hormone.'

I froze instantly. 'What are you saying? That's crazy, I can't be pregnant.'

'Well you need to come in and have some tests done urgently.'

My heart was thumping. 'But I'm out here until just before Christmas, so that's going to be tricky. Can't I just buy a pregnancy test out here?'

'No,' she said, explaining that it could be what's known as an 'incomplete pregnancy', which happens to a lot of women. Without getting too technical, you might have a mini-miscarriage and not even know about it. And if that's happened, a pregnancy test reading would probably still show up as positive. 'So we need to check to see if your levels of HCG are still going up, as that's the important indicator here,' she said.

'But I'm telling you, I can't be pregnant,' I argued. 'I'm on the pill.'

'Well, you still need to get checked over there if you can,' she advised.

So while Matt was having rehab, I called the nearest hospital and explained the situation and booked an appointment for the next morning. After driving there, I was given the blood test – which cost me £250, although at least I did get the results back the same day. And the test showed that my HCG level had shot up even further – to about 40,000 units. The hormone can double every day, apparently.

I called my GP with the results and she said, 'That sounds like you definitely are pregnant. I do think you need to come back home so we can do a dating scan.'

Suddenly, a few things clicked into place: around the time of my birthday a few weeks before, I'd had a lovely night with Matt but I got absolutely paralytic on champagne and wine. And I was so hungover the next morning that I spent all day throwing up. It was probably the worst hangover of my life but, apparently, being ill like that can make your pill completely useless.

While it was totally unexpected, I was secretly thrilled. Matt had only said a couple of nights earlier that we should buy a house together, so the timing seemed perfect. A baby was surely the icing on the cake for us.

I decided to keep it as a surprise for the time being but, when he was safely out having physio, I phoned Mum – who I was finally back on speaking terms with – and blurted out, 'Guess what? I'm pregnant!'

She burst into tears and then I burst into tears.

'That's wonderful news,' she said between sobs. 'I'm so happy for you.'

'Me too,' I said. 'It's the best thing that's happened in months. And I've already thought of how I'm going to break it to Matt. What do you reckon if I put a copy of the baby's scan inside a card for him at Christmas?'

'Sounds like a great idea. He'll be over the moon, won't he?'

'Well, I hope so!'

Reigning myself in from blabbing the news to him was so difficult that I thought I might burst. But I made up an excuse about a big job offer coming in at home and said I had to go back early. He booked me a business-class flight home and, just before I took off, I said, 'I'll miss you loads but it's not long to Christmas now.'

When I got back, I had the dating scan, which showed I was about five weeks gone. They also had to check my ovaries and that the pregnancy wasn't ectopic but, in spite of a few tiny cysts, everything was fine.

'There's nothing to worry about. If anything, it's amazing that you've conceived so easily when you've got polycystic ovaries,' the nurse said.

Feeling elated, I put the copy of the scan in a card, wrapped it up and put it under my Christmas tree along with a load of other presents. I hadn't been this excited about Christmas since I was a little kid.

I don't know if it was just in my head but, by now, I was feeling so sick all the time and all kinds of smells were just vile to me. It didn't matter though – I was so ecstatic about the little baked-bean-sized life form growing in my belly, feeling like death was somehow irrelevant. Matt and I spoke every day and I was counting down the days until he got back. I literally couldn't wait to make my big announcement.

I felt so confident that this was going to be the start of an amazing and positive time for us both. The future was shining more brightly than ever before. Or so I thought.

CHAPTER TWENTY-TWO

Another Betrayal

When Matt flew in from Vermont on 21 December 2009 – the same day as Mum's birthday – he was due to go to a Christmas charity ball with his teammates that night. He'd invited me along weeks before and, though I'd initially said yes, my condition meant that going out partying with a bunch of drunken footballers was the very last thing I could have faced.

'I'm not going to come tonight if that's OK,' I told him when he arrived home. 'I'm not feeling too good.'

'Why? What's wrong?' he said.

'I don't know. I just feel really tired and a bit sick. I think I've got flu coming, which is bloody typical just before Christmas. I'll pick you up though, so you won't have to get a taxi.'

But Matt knew me too well. He could probably tell from 10 paces if I was telling the truth or not. He went quiet for a bit and then said, 'Fine. Whatever.'

Much later, when I picked him up from the black-tie do, he got in the car steaming drunk and in a really odd mood. We drove in silence for a bit and I was feeling strangely apprehensive, although I didn't know why.

'What's really the matter with you?' he said, slurring his words slightly.

'I told you. Just a bit of the flu but it's nothing serious. I'm fine.'

There was another pause and then he just came out with it, brutal and to the point. 'You're pregnant, aren't you?'

I couldn't understand how he'd guessed. 'What? I don't...'

But before I could even get my thoughts together, he butted in, 'You are. Tell me the truth, Chanelle.'

What could I say? It wasn't meant to happen like this at all.

'Well, er... Yes, I am pregnant. But how did you know?'

He just looked at me and I noticed all the colour had drained out of his face. 'What the fuck have you gone and done?'

I couldn't speak. This was a world away from the reaction I was expecting. In my head, I was going to give him the card with the scan in a few days' time and he'd pick me up in his arms and shower me in kisses, saying, 'This is the best news ever!'

We got home and he seemed so angry. He slammed the front door closed and went into the kitchen, opened a bottle of red wine and poured a large glass.

'Why are you cross?' I said, silently crying on the sofa. 'I thought you'd be so happy.'

He sat down in a chair with his legs crossed, swilling around his glass of wine like he was some country gent.

He looked straight at me and his next words tore me apart. 'You did this on purpose. You tricked me into this.'

'No! I swear to God I didn't,' I wept. 'Check my medical records. I didn't have a clue, Matt. I honestly thought you would be pleased. It was meant to be your Christmas present.'

He just shook his head and fixed me with a look of disgust that

I'd never seen on his face before. Although it was very late, he then called his mum, Lesley. This was hardly going to help matters – she had never really liked me, I think because she felt I'd taken her beloved son away from her. He used to visit her almost every day but now he spent all his time with me. I'd always tried to be very polite to her but I sensed she looked down her nose at me.

A little while later, Lesley turned up at the house. 'I told you she would do this, didn't I, Matt?' she glared at me. 'I told you all she wanted was your money.'

I felt my own temper flare then. How dare she say that?

'What are you talking about? I earn a very good living of my own, thanks very much. Do you think I would throw my career away just to live off him? With all his injuries, he might not even be able to play football for much longer.'

'Whatever,' she said. 'You're just a little gold-digger.'

I was absolutely raging by now. 'Lesley, why don't you come round to my house? I've got five bedrooms, a double garage and a huge garden – and I paid for it all myself. I don't need anybody else's money. And even if I didn't have any, I'd have no qualms about cleaning toilets or stacking shelves in Asda. I'm not afraid of hard work.'

Matt said absolutely nothing. He just sat mute in his chair in his beautiful house with his stupid glass of wine.

'You make me sick,' Lesley droned on. 'It was your responsibility to take your pill and you obviously haven't been.'

'What the hell are you talking about? I take it every day. I've actually had extra tests to check that the baby is OK because of the very fact I've been taking the pill.'

Then I turned to Matt. 'Are you going to let her talk to me like this?'

He didn't even look up and I said, 'I can't believe this is happening. I truly thought you wanted this.'

He spoke up at last. 'You tried to kill yourself only a few months ago. Do you seriously think you can look after a child?'

'Yes, I do actually, Matt. This baby is going to mean the world to me.'

He let out a cruel little laugh and shook his head.

At that point, I couldn't stop myself. I jumped forward towards Matt, grabbed the glass from his hand and threw it hard against the wall. Red wine splattered all over his gorgeous luxury wallpaper.

'Fuck you!' I screamed at the top of my lungs. 'If you don't want your child, that's fine but I'm having this baby!'

Lesley piped up again then. 'Who do you think you are?'

'Oh, shut the fuck up,' I snarled. 'You're a nasty, evil bitch.'

Like it was a scene from Jeremy Kyle, I then felt her hand strike me clean across the face and it stung like hell.

I clutched my cheek with my hand and knew I had to get out of there. Grabbing my purse, I pulled out some notes, chucked a load on the floor and, as I walked out the door, said, 'Fix your fucking wallpaper yourself.'

Driving back home down the A1, it was snowing so hard I could hardly see through the windscreen, especially as I was inconsolable at the wheel. At one point I had to pull over to the side of the road because I felt like I was having a panic attack and couldn't breathe. When I got home, I took down my Christmas tree and sobbed myself to sleep. I just felt so horribly sad at how things were unfolding.

The next day, I called Mum and told her what had happened and she was just as gutted as me.

'I genuinely thought he'd be delighted,' she said. 'What are you going to do?'

'This doesn't change a single thing, Mum. I'm keeping the baby and, if Matt doesn't want to know, tough. I'm going to love him or her enough for us both.'

'Well, you know you've got our full support, Chanelle.'

'Thanks, Mum.' That really meant a lot to me.

A few days later, Matt had all my stuff sent to me. He also sent me some particularly nasty text messages. 'I can't believe you trapped me,' he said again. 'Everyone told me not to trust you and that you're devious.'

I calmly replied, 'If that's your take on it, fine. But let's get a few things straight: it takes two people to have sex and two people to make a baby. If you don't want to be around this child, that's fine. But I have suffered for a long time because of the mistakes I've made in the past and you are very wrong if you think I'm going to make another mistake.'

In full flow now, I continued, 'I will be a brilliant mum and give this child a good upbringing. If you don't want to be involved, that's your choice. But don't bother sending me abuse becaµse you're not going to change my mind.'

It was so strange – we never sat down and had a proper, rational conversation about our options – just that nightmarish fight and then a string of these horrible texts.

Quite why he was so against having the baby I'll never know. But I think it probably all boiled down to money, plain and simple. Of course, lots of girls get pregnant so they can get themselves a nice house to live in but I had one of my own. And he should have known me well enough to know that I'm not one of those sponging trollops who target rich footballers so they don't ever have to do an honest day's work again. My strong work ethic is one of the things I'm most proud of. I was brought up to be like that and, even though Dad has always worked hard as a graphic designer, he also does social work on the side. He and Mum are natural grafters and they definitely instilled that principle in me. So what Matt and his spiteful mum were accusing me of was so far wide of the mark.

I can't lie though – my pregnancy was very tough. For the first three months I was so sick I couldn't eat anything without throwing up. I lost about a stone and a half and had to be rehydrated at hospital a few times and some nights I slept on the sofa because I was too weak to get up the stairs. One of the only things I could eat without being sick was Haribo cola bottles – they were so sour that they didn't even taste like food.

When I later went for a 3D scan with Mum, I told the nurse doing the ultrasound, 'I reckon it's a girl because, apparently, you get more sick with girls. And believe me, I've been so, so sick.'

'Well, let's find out if your theory is correct, shall we?' she said with a grin.

And then, as the mesmerising image of my baby came up on the monitor, she said, 'I've got some news for you. It's a boy!'

'You're kidding?' I exclaimed. 'I'd have put my mortgage on it being a girl!'

'No, look – there's its little willy,' she said pointing to the screen.

'Are you sure that's not an umbilical cord?'

'No, it's definitely a willy.'

We all laughed. I was so certain I was having a girl that I'd been planning a pink nursery, so this was quite a surprise. But as I got used to the idea, I felt really pleased – boys were surely far easier and less complicated than girls, after all!

Not only was I poorly for months on end but I was going through it alone. Matt and I were hardly speaking and the only contact we had was via awkward text messages. A few months into my pregnancy, it struck me that I was going to need a bigger car when the baby arrived, as I only had a tiny Mini, which was highly impractical for lugging around kids' stuff. I knew that Matt was in the process of buying a new Bentley and I had this genius idea that I could borrow his old BMW for a while, once

I'd given birth. Surely that was the least he could do for his own child.

I texted him to ask if that would be possible one Friday afternoon, while I was waiting at the doctor's surgery for a pregnancy check-up. His reply shot back straight away: 'You've got a nerve. I knew it wouldn't be long until you started asking me for everything.'

I was flabbergasted. 'But it'd only be a loan. We can draw up a contract to say that I'll give the car back again when I've gone back to work.'

'My mum was right,' he wrote. 'She warned me you'd be like this.'

This was ludicrous. 'Matt, what am I supposed to do? Shove the baby on the roof of my Mini with the pushchair sticking out the window? I need a bigger car and your BMW is going to be sitting on your driveway, not even being used.'

'I'm giving it to my mum,' he said.

So that's what it all came down to. 'Well, if you're that bothered, your mum can have my Mini for a year and then, when the baby is old enough to sit in the front, we can swap back again.'

As our messages went back and forth, he then said, 'I'll get you a new car – a Fiesta for £600.'

This comment really upset me – how could he even think of letting his own son or daughter be driven around in a heap of junk?

'Matt, I could buy a car like that myself but I don't think it would be safe for me to drive our child around in some rust bucket.'

His next reply was even more painful: 'Gone are the days when you were earning more than me so, if I don't want to give you a car, I won't give.'

Even though I was in a public waiting room, I'd started to cry and my tears were still streaming when I was called in to see the doctor. She took one look at me and said, 'What on earth is going on?'

I told her what had just happened and the whole story came tumbling out as I sobbed hysterically. You know when you're just gulping in air because you're so upset? That's exactly how I was.

'I feel like I'm all on my own,' I cried. 'I just feel like I can't cope and that I need more support. What am I going to do?'

She listened to me talk and, as I started to pull myself together, fetched me a glass of water.

'I'm so sorry about all of that,' I said. 'The timing was just really unfortunate. We'd been having it out right there in the waiting room. It was so hurtful and I just needed to get it off my chest.'

She looked at me with a concerned expression but said nothing.

'I think it's just hit me that I really am going to be a single parent and that it's going to be incredibly tough.'

Finally, she spoke – and her response wasn't what I was expecting. 'Chanelle, what are you saying? Do you think you're going to harm yourself or the baby?'

'No! Of course not,' I said incredulously. 'I'm just feeling a bit overwhelmed at the moment but I'll be fine. I'd never harm my baby.'

I will never forgive her as long as I live for what she did next.

'I'm sorry, Chanelle but I don't feel confident about that. After what you did last summer, I can't be sure you won't do something rash again. Therefore, I cannot allow you to leave this appointment.'

What the actual hell? Were my ears deceiving me?

'I'm afraid I have no choice but to section you under the Mental Health Act.'

My eyes must have looked like they were out on stalks. Did she actually just say that? I was utterly horrified.

'Don't be so ridiculous,' I snapped. 'You can't section me! I'm just going to drive home now – I'm fine! I came to you for some support but that doesn't mean I'm going to do something stupid.'

'But I can't take that risk,' she said. 'It's my duty to protect you and your baby.'

I had known this woman for years – she was like a friend to me, so this seemed like some sick, very unfunny joke.

'Oh my God, do you actually think I'm going to go and stab myself in the stomach or get in a hot bath with a coat-hanger and a bottle of gin? This is bullshit.'

I stood up to leave but she said, 'I'm sorry, Chanelle. You can't go anywhere. I really do have to section you.'

'Well, how are you going to do that? You can't physically drag me there yourself. I want to go home, right now.'

'That's not possible, Chanelle. I've already told the reception staff to call an ambulance and a community police officer will be here soon, in case you refuse to go.'

This was simply unbelievable. I was about to be taken off to a padded cell, just for getting upset over a fight with my unborn child's father. Hardly a sign of raving bloody insanity, was it?

Trying not to let the panic show in my voice, I said, 'I need to phone my parents. Let me speak to them.'

She did, at least, allow me to make the call but Mum was so stunned that she passed me on to Dad, who clearly didn't fully understand the severity of my situation.

'Well, there's nothing we can do if you've gone in there in such a state, is there? Just get yourself checked over and I'm sure it'll all be fine later.'

Great! Thanks for that, Dad. Really helpful. So I phoned my

mum's sister, my Aunty Susan, who is one of the nicest people in the world. She and Mum finish each other's sentences and probably speak five times a day and I love her to bits. In fact, she and my Uncle Paul are just like Mum and Dad but from a different village.

Anyway, Aunty Susan said she'd come straight to the doctor's but, by the time she arrived, it was too late. I'd been carted out and taken by ambulance to Fieldhead Hospital, in Wakefield – a renowned mental-health facility. I know it sounds awful but Fieldhead used to be the butt of our jokes at school. It was known as the local loony bin; where all the crazy people go – and now I was being treated like one of them.

The paramedic led me out of the doctor's by my arm and I tried to shrug him off, saying, 'Why are you doing that? I'm perfectly capable to walk by myself.'

'Well, you've been sectioned,' he said. 'You might be a little unstable.'

'I certainly am not unstable,' I replied. 'I just happen to be pregnant and have an ex-boyfriend who's being a bastard. But if we'd had this argument yesterday, you wouldn't even know about it.'

'I'm sorry,' he said, 'but there's nothing you can do and, if you resist coming with us, you'll be arrested.'

Over at Fieldhead, I was admitted to a tiny, claustrophobic room, which could make even the sanest person alive feel like some kind of lunatic. It was terrifying. I sat there for six hours in a room with no windows, no light switches and nothing remotely sharp. There wasn't even a handle on my side of the door. Everything was smooth and flat so you couldn't hurt yourself.

My Aunty Susan eventually turned up but I told her to go home, as they'd said it would be hours until I was assessed. And I just sat on the bed thinking, 'What did I do in a previous life to deserve this?' There was a camera in the room focused on me all the time and, despite me being about 20 weeks pregnant, I was given nothing to eat all day. All I had was a glass of water and nobody came to see if I was OK. That really was enough to send you stir crazy.

Eventually, this nice doctor with kind eyes came to assess me. He asked me a ton of questions, like, 'How are you feeling?' and, 'How do you feel about your baby?'

I basically told him what I'd said to my GP – albeit in a much calmer manner – and that I would never harm my child in a billion years.

After a few seconds, he stood up and said, 'Well, I'm very sorry but you shouldn't have been brought here. We need to get you discharged as soon as possible.' Thank Christ someone had a bit of common sense here! 'It was obviously a very extreme measure and all I can do is apologise.'

'Thank you,' I said, so grateful I could have hugged him. 'I know it's nothing to do with you but the way I've been treated is a complete disgrace.'

He nodded. 'I will follow it up because it's been a waste of our time too and taken up a room that we could potentially have assigned to another patient.'

Looking back on that encounter, I'm still appalled by it. I know the NHS is brilliant and I've always championed it but, to this day, I can't understand how I was put in that position. I guess my doctor was only trying to cover her own back because, if I had done something silly, it would have been a big news story. She was probably on red alert because it had been in the papers when I'd tried to kill myself the summer before. So I do understand it from her point of view, but to be dragged off to a mental institution like that was an epic overreaction. I have suffered minor bouts of depression since then but now I would never go and see a GP about it because I'm sure they'd try and make out I was clinically insane again. I've lost trust in the system, which is such a shame.

The doctor told me I was free to leave but it wasn't that simple. 'My car is still at the doctor's,' I said. 'And all my money and my house keys are in my bag, which I locked in the boot.'

'Right,' said the doctor. 'We'll have to get you a police escort home then.'

That was a shambles too because, when the police car pulled up at the surgery, the gates to the car park were locked.

'I have to get those gates open,' I told him. 'I can't get into my house otherwise.'

Glancing up at the barbed wire reeled across the gates, the policeman said, 'Nope, you won't be getting in there tonight. Can you stay elsewhere?'

He took me to my neighbour Lisa's house and, sometime later, Mum dropped off a spare set of house keys. What a nightmare day. In the four years since then, I've only ever told a couple of my friends about it because I found the whole thing so embarrassing and demeaning. And I never told Matt because I was certain he would have really gone to town with it.

Still, as I was soon to discover, my troubles with him were far from over.

CHAPTER TWENTY-THREE

Friends In Need

About five months into my pregnancy, when I was feeling rotten, alone and very vulnerable, I had a surprising and very random text from this guy called Jack Tweed. He'd become quite well known, mostly because he was married to Jade Goody. Jade was a former *Big Brother* housemate like me and had died tragically of cervical cancer on Mother's Day the previous year, leaving behind two young sons, Freddie and Bobby. She died just six weeks after marrying Jack and he was completely devastated by it.

Jack had worked in nightclub promotion and I'd seen him around at events once or twice in the past but that was all. He was best mates with *TOWIE's* Mark Wright, although that show hadn't even started by this point. I wasn't really a fan of that whole Essex crowd though and I used to see Mark a lot in Embassy nightclub because he was friends with the guys at Neon Management, my agency. I personally found Mark really sleazy. He was always offering to buy me drinks but I thought he was a bit of wet lettuce and looked really old!

Jack, who was six months older than me, had got my number from one of the agents at Neon and his first text hardly blew me away: 'Alright, babe?' it said.

'Er, hi,' I replied. 'Whose number is this?'

'It's Jack Tweed. What are you up to?'

'Nothing much.'

What else could I say? It was extremely weird but we carried on texting – just inane banter to begin with but, as I said, I was lonely and craving company. Being pregnant, I was knackered a lot of the time and every day at 5pm I'd lie on the sofa and watch *Deal or No Deal*. Then Jack started watching it too at his home down in Essex and we'd text back and forth all the way through it.

It had been reported in the celeb mags by now that I was pregnant with Matt's child and I assumed Jack knew. But it turns out he had no idea. Because I'd been so sick in the early stages of pregnancy, I was still hardly showing, so I looked totally normal in recent photos. People had even accused me of faking the whole baby thing for publicity. As if I'd be so desperate to do anything like that.

But I was also clueless about what was going on in Jack's life at the time. I had no idea he was up on a rape charge. Perhaps I'd been living in a bubble with all the drama in my own life but, somehow, this news had passed me by.

As our friendly text exchanges continued, I mentioned to Jack that I was going to London for a couple of days on a photo-shoot and he said, 'Can I take you out for a meal when you're down?'

'I'm not sure, I'll have to think about it,' I said. It really was an odd situation to find myself in and I couldn't work out how I felt about it.

I turned to Mum for some advice: 'Do you think it would be really bad if I went out on a date while I'm pregnant?'

She thought for about a couple of seconds. 'You've had nothing but misery lately. Why not go out and have some fun? Let someone make you feel nice and special for a change.'

So I agreed and, on the day of our 'date', Jack said he'd pick me up from my friend Jenny's in London at 1.30pm. But he was really late and turned up in a taxi.

'Erm, where's your car?' I said.

'Oh, yeah, I don't drive. I thought we could go out in your car.'

Great start, Jack. He'd also turned up in a flat cap and he was clutching a huge golfing umbrella. He looked daft and straight away I started taking the mickey out of him.

'Going for the country-gent look, are you?' I joked. 'Anyway, where are we going?'

'London Zoo.'

When we got there, it was pouring with rain, so we didn't stay long. As we got back in my car, a text beeped in from his mum, Mary. He read it and then said slowly, 'Are you pregnant?'

'Er, yes,' I replied. 'About five months. Did you not know? I thought you would have Googled me before we met up.'

'Well, I think my mum's just been Googling you.'

Trying to carry on the date as normally as possible, we went to Camden Market. I was trying to make casual conversation and he bought me a body scrub – which I hate because it rubs my fake tan off!

Then we went to Gilgamesh, a trendy Asian restaurant, for an early dinner, at which point Jack said, 'Do you mind if my friends join us?'

'No, that's fine,' I said, quite relieved to have other people around to help break the ice.

When his mates showed up, it was Arg and Lydia from *TOWIE*. My first thought was how enormous Arg was but they were really nice and we ended up having a good time.

I dropped them all home in Essex and later Jack sent me a brief, formal text: 'Thanks for the lift.'

'Hmm,' I thought. 'This is never going to go anywhere'.

I didn't realise he was quite shy at that point but he texted again later. 'I wanted to give you a kiss goodbye but I was too embarrassed in front of Arg and Lydia. Do you think you might come down again?'

This was a turn-up for the books. 'I didn't think you'd had a good time,' I said.

'No, I enjoyed myself. Why don't you come down to our house and stay some time?'

I said I'd think about it. I still had no idea that Jack was facing criminal charges and it was only when I was telling Zoe about my day out that I discovered what was going on.

'You do know that Jack's going on trial for rape, don't you?' Zoe said.

'What are you on about?' I said, thinking it couldn't be true. It was certainly not something Jack was singing from the rooftops. But I went online and saw exactly what Zoe was talking about. Back in September 2009, Jack and his friend Anthony had been accused by a teenage girl of taking her from a London club back home to Essex and then forcing themselves on her. Soon after I met Jack, they were both acquitted for rape but, by then, he'd spent a lot of time on remand in Pentonville Prison, a harrowing experience that affected him terribly. He was severely bullied by the other prisoners and one of them even threatened to steal his wedding ring. In later months, Jack told how he was so destroyed by his time in jail that he contemplated suicide. 'If I'd had a gun, I would have shot myself in the head without a question,' he said. 'I couldn't handle it.'

When I came into the picture, Jack was still awaiting the trial and, though he didn't ever want to talk about it, I really felt for him and what he was going through. As far as I was concerned, everyone is innocent until proven guilty – and the guy I was getting to know didn't appear capable of rape at all. To me, he seemed quite gentle and lost, like a little boy. Despite winning the case, it was a bit of a hollow victory for Jack, as the whole case had understandably ruined his life. People still call him a rapist today, despite the fact that he walked out a free man. It's such a vile word and I know how sensitive he is about it. Sadly, mud sticks though, regardless of him being acquitted. I think it's appalling that Jack still feels the weight of the trial.

Jack's situation when I was getting to know him meant that he had to wear a police tag and stick to strict curfews at home. It made sense then that he'd asked me to go down to Essex and stay with him. I agreed to go because I felt he needed some support – and, let's face it, so did I.

I know some people think I was mad for getting involved with someone awaiting trial for such a serious crime but we were both so fucked up. He was still heartbroken after losing Jade and I was heartbroken because I'd split up with my long-term boyfriend and the father of my unborn child. We both just craved love and some stability so, in some ways, we were perfect for each other.

Hopefully, this explains why we just jumped into it straight away. We were both needy and scared of being on our own. My confidence was also desperately low and, being pregnant and on my own, my options seemed frighteningly limited. I feared no guy would ever accept me with someone else's child in tow.

When I went down to his family's home in Essex, I met his mum Mary and dad, Andy, and they were so welcoming. Mary got me a jar of pickles, in case I was craving them (although I wasn't) and she'd bought new bedding from John Lewis for the spare room, where I was obviously sleeping on my own.

The morning after I arrived, Jack went to the gym and, as I sat down at the table with Mary, she said, 'Jack's never taken any girl out on a date apart from Jade. He obviously likes you.' Apparently this was true – although he'd been with a lot of girls, he never took them for a meal or anything.

Of course, we'd had to broach the subject of me being pregnant. Although Jack didn't want to dwell on it, he seemed completely OK with it – probably because I told him I didn't speak to the baby's dad any more. I suppose he wasn't fazed either because he'd spent so long with Jade and her boys, whose dad was the reality-TV star Jeff Brazier.

The second evening I was there, Jack's friends all came round to the house because his electronic tag meant he couldn't stay out late. They put on a bit of an impromptu karaoke party and everyone had a go at singing, even his mum and dad. It was a lovely, fun night.

When I left to go back home after a couple of days, Jack walked me to my car and that's when we had our first kiss. It felt right. But in case you're wondering, we never slept together at all while I was pregnant – I think that would have been disgusting. It never really came up in conversation and, despite his reputation, I think Jack did have respect for me on that matter – even if it was frustrating for him.

After that visit, I started spending a lot of time with Jack in Essex, usually around three days of every week. We were getting on really well but, on one occasion, I had a shocking scare while I was with him and his family. Still in my own separate bedroom, I woke up to find the sheets stained with blood. It was so frightening. I was convinced I was having a miscarriage. Shaking with fear, I woke Jack's mum and she drove me straight to hospital. When we got there, I was silent and just felt like an empty shell. If I lost my baby, my life may as well be over too.

There were several other people waiting in A&E but I was rushed straight to the front of the queue. You always know it's bad when that happens and straight away I was hooked up to a load of monitors. Pretty quickly, the doctors told me I'd gone into very early labour and that there was no way the baby could survive being born at this stage. They started giving me steroids to try and stop the labour, which they said was happening because, for some inexplicable reason, my body was trying to get rid of the baby.

Although Jack couldn't face coming to the hospital after what he'd been through during Jade's illness the previous year, Mary and Andy were complete lifesavers. They brought me food in a picnic basket at every mealtime and Mary sat chatting with me and reassuring me for hours on end. I've never met two people who were so selfless and, when Mum dashed down to see me, they welcomed her into their home and drove her back and forth to the hospital every day. I can never thank them enough for that.

When the drugs began to take hold, the labour process stopped and the doctors' visits became less and less frequent, which I took to be a good sign. Eventually, after five agonising days, one of the female specialists came to see me and said, 'Everything is fine. You are going to be a high-risk pregnancy from now on but the baby is fine.'

Those were surely the greatest words I'd ever heard. 'Thank you so much for saving my baby,' I sobbed with relief. 'I'll always be grateful.'

'You're welcome,' she said with a smile. 'You can go home now but you mustn't do any strenuous activity or allow any knocks to your stomach.'

'Of course not,' I vowed. Nothing was going to harm my baby now. All the time I'd been in hospital I'd been feeling guilty that perhaps doing a few gentle routines with my personal trainer while pregnant had brought on the labour. After that scare, I decided I'd never risk it again.

Soon afterwards, I had another bleeding episode during a photo-shoot with *new!* magazine. It was then that I knew I had to slow down with work too. Waking up at 3am to drive down to London and not getting back until 11pm was too much. My body was clearly telling me, 'Stop now.'

At that point, I decided not to stay down in Essex any more either. I needed to be near my own friends and family. It was hard because it meant I'd see much less of Jack but I had to put my baby first.

As I'd feared though, my moving back up north full time soon began to take a toll on our relationship. On the one hand, he'd send me lovely, caring texts and, on the occasions he came up to Wakefield, he'd tenderly kiss my stomach as if he imagined it was his baby inside. It felt lovely to know someone wanted this child with me. And I knew he deeply missed seeing Jade's sons, Freddie and Bobby.

But on the flip side, things would be dreadful between us at other times because, when he was back in Essex, he'd go out, get drunk and cop off with some girl in a club on a Friday night. I'd read about it in the papers and online and go mad but he'd always come back to me, saying how sorry he was. I felt I couldn't really judge him because we weren't living together in any normal capacity and, after being found not-guilty in the rape ordeal, he needed to let loose. That was his coping mechanism. But as you can see, it was hardly a fairy-tale romance.

As I settled into the late stages of pregnancy, I suddenly blew up like a bouncy castle and became absolutely gigantic! I'd been so teeny in the beginning but now I was wearing huge maternity clothes. I joked that my arms looked like legs and my face looked like my arse! And although my shoe size is normally a five, I was wearing size-seven flip-flops at my baby shower. But even then the bloody things burst open under the pressure of my swollen toes!

My expanding bump caused chronic sciatica, which ruined a holiday in Greece with my friend Jenny. The plan was to have a last-minute bit of R&R but I cried for five days non-stop because my back was so bad. I couldn't lie down or get up, or even go to the toilet.

Getting so big and out of my comfort zone was tough and often downright painful but it was funny, in a way, because my attitude towards my body completely changed. In the past, I would have rather died than look like the heifer I'd become but I'd realised it wasn't about me any more. There was another life inside me and that was all that mattered. I still feel that way now as a mum. Being a bit heavier these days is a small price to pay for having a child and nowadays I never get too hung up on it. Quite simply, motherhood is the greatest gift in life and, if that means carrying a few extra pounds, so be it!

CHAPTER TWENTY-FOUR

Welcome to the World!

While Matt and I had not been in contact through most of the pregnancy, there was a surprising and dramatic twist to the tale when one day I got a blunt text from him, saying, 'How are things with the pregnancy? I'd like to be there at the birth and for the baby's surname to be Bates. Please can you contact me about this?'

It was so bizarre because, until that point, I'd always let him know the time and dates of my scans and appointments but he had never turned up. It didn't seem like he was interested in the various pictures I'd sent him either. So when this message pinged in, I was knocked for six. I was with Rachel, who was also pregnant, and we sat looking at each other in amazement.

'I don't believe this,' I said to her. 'I feel like I'm going crazy. One minute he wants nothing to do with the baby and now he's saying he wants to be involved.' It's almost like he had a dual personality because, from that moment, he became very civil and took a big interest in what was going on. I felt though that his request to be at the birth was inappropriate, especially as I'd already decided that Mum was going to be my birthing partner.

I told him, 'You're more than welcome to come to the hospital after I've given birth but I don't want you there during it.'

He wasn't happy about this but I said, 'That's my decision but I'm very happy for you to establish a relationship with your son if that's what you want.'

Trying to read what was going on inside his head, I can only assume that he suddenly thought, 'What can I do? She really is having this baby.' Whatever switch had flipped in his brain meant he was now also keen for our child to take his surname, which inevitably jarred with me.

'I don't want it to have the name Bates because you haven't been around for most of the pregnancy,' I said, which was surely a fair point.

But he wouldn't let it go, saying it was only correct and proper that the baby takes the father's name. I suppose I was so relieved that he was getting involved at long last that I relented a bit.

'OK, listen,' I said. 'If you agree to having weekly, regular contact with the baby and to playing a proper part in his life, we'll give him a double-barrelled surname. It can be Hayes-Bates.'

'No way,' he said. 'I just want Bates.'

It was so exasperating. You could tell he got paid a lot of money and was used to getting his own way.

'I'm trying to meet you in the middle here,' I said. 'It's either going to be double-barrelled or it's just going to be Hayes.'

'OK then,' he huffed. 'Double-barrelled. What's his first name going to be?'

This was a good question. Over the past few months, I'd spent at least £200 on baby-name books and had them scattered all over my living-room floor, like it was some massively important science experiment. I'd always really liked old English names but I knew I

WELCOME TO THE WORLD!

wanted one that was unusual. I definitely didn't want a run-of-the-mill name, partly because I'd always loved being the only Chanelle in my peer group. At school there had been about 10 girls called Sarah in my year and everyone was forever mixing them up.

One name I'd stumbled on was 'Blakely'. I really liked it because it was unique but sounded very traditional and English. Other contenders I had up my sleeve were 'Caesar' and 'Fabian' – which, looking back, would have been absolutely horrendous choices! I even considered calling him 'Winter' but Zoe wisely stepped in at that point and said, 'Over my dead body, Chanelle. You are not calling your child Winter Hayes!'

Blakely seemed a good option because it definitely didn't sound chavvy and I thought he could also shorten it to Blake when he's grown up. But when I told Matt this was my preferred choice, he said, 'It sounds stupid.'

Like he really had a say in this. 'I don't care what you think,' I said angrily. 'I've bought all the baby's stuff – his pram, the cot, a changing table, toys, murals and everything, while you've not contributed at all. You've made my pregnancy awful. And now you want to sit there and dictate what he's going to be called? I don't think so, Matt. I like the name Blakely and that's final.'

As I approached my due date that August, I was filled with anxiety about childbirth and was fairly certain that I'd die during it. So imagine how relieved I was when it was all done and dusted in two and a half hours! It all began in the early hours of 20 July 2010, when I woke up and was so uncomfortable I knew I wasn't going to be able to get back to sleep. My TV was still on, so I plumped up my pillows a bit and started watching an episode of *South Park*.

Then, as I wriggled around a bit, I suddenly felt that the sheets were all soggy underneath me.

'Oh my God, I've wet the bed!' I said out loud, even though I

CHANELLE HAYES – BARING MY HEART

was completely alone in the house. Jack hadn't been to see me for ages because he knew Matt was back in touch and he hated to even hear a mention of his name. We were very much going through one of our 'off' phases – he seemed more concerned with having a good time with his mates and getting lashed every night. Whatever – I had far more important things to think about.

Losing control of my bladder was the final straw with the pregnancy. What a nightmare. I manoeuvred myself out of bed to go to the bathroom but, when I stood up, all this liquid came flooding out.

'That's not wee,' I thought instinctively. I assumed my waters must have broken but I wasn't sure if that meant I should be getting my stuff and heading to hospital just yet. I sat Googling it for half an hour and then called Mum and Dad.

I figured they wouldn't be best pleased if this was a false alarm, since they'd taken me to hospital only the day before. I hadn't felt the baby move for 24 hours, so was panicking that something was badly wrong. The doctors had me hooked up to a monitor for hours but, thankfully, everything had been OK.

When I called Mum and Dad this time, it took them ages to answer the phone – but then it was about 4am, so that was understandable. Mum eventually answered and I said, 'Sorry, I know you only took me to hospital yesterday but I need to go again. Right now.'

'Listen, sweetheart,' she said. 'I think you need to stop worrying. The baby is fine. You don't need to go back.'

'No, listen to me. My waters have broken, Mum.'

'What? OK, why didn't you say? Right. Wait there. We'll be round in five minutes!'

Unhelpfully, there was a terrible storm raging that night and Dad didn't want to take the motorway to hospital, even though that was the quickest route.

'Shall we go the long way round?' he said once they'd picked me up.

'No way!' I yelled from the back seat of the car. 'Who do you think we are? Mary and Joseph riding on a donkey? Just hurry up and get me there!'

So we piled on to the motorway and Dad crawled along at about 20mph as the rain and gale-force winds lashed down at us. The journey usually takes 20 minutes but, because of the bad weather, it took double that. While poor Dad struggled to see out of the windscreen with the wipers on full pelt, I was having contractions in the back and writhing in agony and Mum was holding my hand, saying, 'Calm down, dear.' It was like *Carry on Camping* with a bit of childbirth thrown in.

When we arrived, we charged into the maternity unit and the staff said, 'Oh, Chanelle, you're back.'

'Yeah, sorry,' I said. 'But this time I think I'm in labour!'

A nurse checked me over and said, 'Yes, you're four-centimetres dilated. That's probably what yesterday was all about. The baby was probably having a big rest before he came out.'

Despite that, she said I was still hours away from giving birth, so I sent Dad home to get me some clothes and make-up. Because the baby technically hadn't been due for three more weeks, I hadn't had a bag packed ready, so I was sitting there barefaced and in my pyjamas. I'd not yet had my roots or bikini line done either, so I couldn't have looked worse if I'd tried!

About an hour after we got to the hospital, my contractions started getting much stronger and much more painful. Surely this wasn't supposed to happen if I was still ages away from the birth? The nurses had even assured me that nothing would happen until the next shift of staff clocked on a few hours later.

Although the pain was like nothing I'd ever experienced before, I managed to stay really calm while all of this was going on. Mum even said, 'I wish I'd videoed this – nobody will ever believe it!'

She was the most fantastic birthing partner I could ever have wished for, handing me cold flannels, giving me little sips of water and rubbing my back. It was all new to her too – she'd never given birth herself, so God knows how it came so naturally to her. If she hadn't been there, I really don't know what I'd have done. It proved to me more than ever what an amazing woman she is.

As the contractions intensified, the nurses gave me gas and air but that made me feel sick. So then they gave me an injection for the pain but it was too late because, literally a few minutes afterwards, the baby came! The drugs didn't actually kick in until after the birth, so that was a bit pointless and I felt stoned all morning.

Baby Blakely was born at 6.04am, weighing 6lbs 9oz. He was so small but the doctors told me that, if I had gone to full-term, he might have been 11lbs. I'd have never been able to walk again! When they placed this tiny bundle in my arms, I turned to Mum and said, 'He looks like a cooked chicken!'

Of course, I was filled with instant love and fascination for Blakely but I didn't immediately think, 'How gorgeous is he?' I wanted to cuddle him because he was mine but, if I'm totally honest, I don't think new-born babies are that cute. They have a hard time getting out into the world – it's like running a marathon, so they're not going to look their best!

My other thought when he'd been born was how much he looked like his dad. He was like this tiny version of Matt staring up at me, which was more than a little disconcerting.

Soon after, Dad arrived back with all my clothes and make-up. He was walking along the corridor in the maternity unit and heard these ear-splitting screams and thought to himself, 'That's Chanelle, showing herself up again.' But it was actually the woman in the next room he could hear. I was sitting there all serene and spaced out with Blakely in my arms!

When he walked in, he dropped my bag, took one look at us both and said, 'It's a real baby!' Then he just dissolved into tears. It was so sweet, especially because he rarely shows any emotion. He and Mum had adopted me when I was a few months old and then David when he was nearly two, so they'd never really been around new-born babies. I was over the moon that he was so happy because, when I first told him I was pregnant, let's just say he wasn't exactly delirious with joy. He thought that Matt and I should have been married if we were going to have a child together. But life doesn't always work out like that, does it?

Mum and Dad were besotted with their grandson from the word go and would endlessly squabble over who got to hold him, feed him or wash him. It was hilarious. Even now they spoil Blakely rotten and it gets on my nerves because, when he comes home to me, he really acts up. I'm constantly saying, 'No!' whereas he always gets his own way with his grandma and granddad. They tell me off for being a mini-Hitler at home but I don't ever want him to turn into a little brat like I was.

Although I was gutted that I'd not had time to change my clothes or do my hair and make-up in time for his grand entrance into the world, it was a very special and unique time to be in that little room with Mum, Dad and Blakely. The only thing missing was his father Matt.

Half an hour after the birth, I'd texted Matt, who was away with his club in Germany. 'I've had the baby,' I wrote. 'The labour was only a couple of hours, so you wouldn't have made it back. But we're both fine.'

I didn't expect it but he jumped on a flight back almost immediately and was still in his football kit when he turned up at the hospital. He genuinely seemed to be very excited, which hurts me even more now I know how things turned out.

Holding Blakely in his arms, it was as if we were normal

parents embarking on a miraculous journey as a new family. He didn't want to put Blakely down and gazed at him with big puppy-dog eyes. In those first couple of days, he seemed full of love for his son and would insist on bathing and changing him. I had to stay in hospital for five days because Blakely had arrived three weeks early and Matt came to visit every day, bringing me snacks and supplies for the baby and generally acting the way any new dad would. He'd even give me cuddles and say to Blakely, 'Isn't she a good mummy?'

When I was finally allowed to leave hospital, we took Blakely back to my place together. That was obviously quite emotional because it's a really big deal for new parents to take their baby home for the first time. I found it all very confusing, simply because he had wanted nothing to do with either of us for so long.

Matt took what seemed like hundreds of photos of Blakely and made me an album of his first week, with his tiny footprint in it. He really seemed keen to be part of his life at last and I was so pleased. Not because I wanted to be with Matt myself but because I truly didn't want our son to have a dysfunctional family life.

As he was spending so much time with us both, Matt asked if he could move back in for a few weeks, which I agreed to – though we stayed in separate bedrooms. There was no question of anything happening between us; I was just a new mum in need of all the help I could get and full of relief that he'd come back into the fold.

We blindly navigated our way through those early days of parenthood and, despite our cluelessness and the inevitable sleepless nights, Matt loved doing the night feeds and went out of his way to do his bit around the house too.

We'd surely weathered the worst storm possible: what could go wrong now?

CHAPTER TWENTY-FIVE

Money Talks

Matt and I were getting on fine in the beginning. It was good to have him in the house sharing baby duties and, bit by bit, we were learning the ropes of being parents. Admittedly, it was awkward when his mum Lesley came to visit because I hadn't seen her since that horrible day when we'd screamed at each other until we were blue in the face.

She'd barely walked in the front door before she said, 'This is a big house for just you, isn't it?'

I'd run out of patience with her biting remarks. 'Well, I've paid for it all if that's what you're thinking,' I snapped.

'Oh, I didn't mean anything by it. I was just saying.'

She sat on one side of the sofa and my parents were on the other. You could have cut the atmosphere with a knife.

Then she said, 'I hope Blakely grows up to look like Matt – although I can tell he already looks like you.'

I just smiled and gritted my teeth. I didn't want a scene this time. But in spite of my intentions to stay on good terms with her, she was at the heart of a bitter row which blew up between Matt and I about a month after Blakely was born.

Things had been working OK. We didn't talk about the future, mainly because nursing a baby during those first few weeks is all-consuming and exhausting. Matt was also commuting to Middlesbrough at the same time, so we were both constantly shattered. It wasn't any great surprise then when we started bickering again. One day, we were arguing about something really trivial – like whose turn it was to tidy up – and I lost my temper with him for no real reason.

'I'm sorry but you buggered off for nine months and didn't want to know and now you've jumped in like you're bloody "Superdad".'

'You're such a moody cow,' he said. 'And you're not even trying to lose your baby weight.'

This was a truly low blow. 'I'm sorry but Blakely is only a few weeks old! If I want to sit here and eat a Big Mac, I'll eat ten of them, thanks very much. Who are you to criticise me? We're not even together, are we?' He looked at me blankly. 'Or are you telling me you do want to be together?' I asked. 'You just don't make it clear.'

'For fuck's sake,' he said. 'It's always got to be about you, hasn't it?'

I'd had enough then. 'Right, Matt, I think it's time for you to move out. You're not staying here any more. If you want to see Blakely, you can drive down every day. Normally, people wouldn't be this accommodating after what you did.'

This really upset him. 'But I won't see Blakely as much. You can't do that. It's not fair.' I couldn't believe it but he was almost crying.

'People who break up don't just live together again because they've had a baby. That's not how the world works,' I said. 'We need a schedule and we need to stick to it.'

He stood up then and left and we didn't speak for a couple of days. After he'd cooled off, he called me and said, 'If you won't let me stay at yours, I'll buy an apartment down there. Then I can have Blakely for half of the week.'

He had to be joking, right? Trying to contain myself, I said, 'That's a really nice gesture, Matt, but you can't have him for half the week. That was never the plan.'

'But that's my right as his dad,' he argued.

Getting angry now, I said, 'But you were not even around during the pregnancy. You can't have joint custody. That's not on. Besides, what will happen to him when you have to go off training every day?'

'My mum will look after him,' he said.

'Your mother? No way. She was so mean to me if you remember. She's not bringing him up four mornings a week when I, his own mum, am available to do it. Do you really think I'd sit at home twiddling my thumbs while Blakely goes to your mum's? I don't think so. I want to spend every second with him.'

'Well, so do I,' he said.

We went round and round in circles but, eventually, he dropped the whole issue and decided not to buy a place near me after all. Peace was restored. Over the next few months, he carried on visiting Blakely several days a week – usually in the evenings, as he liked bathing him and putting him to bed. We settled into this routine and it was strange because he seemed to like spending time with me too. Even after Blakely was asleep, he'd sit on the sofa with me and watch TV for an hour or two. It was weirdly comfortable.

By the time Christmas 2010 came around and Blakely was a bit older, the three of us often went on little days out together. We'd go shopping and Matt would buy me a new outfit or book me in for a massage while he looked after Blakely. We even took him to see Santa, which was such a family thing to do. Matt really did seem to adore his son and spoiled him rotten for his first Christmas, showering him with expensive presents. I'd spent a small fortune on him too, so my whole living room was filled with gifts, which, of course, he didn't really need at six months old!

I know I've painted a harmonious picture but it was difficult to carry on as we were, because Jack was still vaguely on the scene too. I say vaguely, because, although he'd been up to see me and Blakely a few times, he was still going out partying down in Essex. He smoked a lot of weed with his mates too, which I always found revolting, and I wanted nothing to do with his 'other' life. He could morph into a different person when he got drunk and it led to us having some vicious fights on Twitter. One time, he even posted up a photo of a girl's boobs and then of some nasty tart giving me the finger. I found it so disgusting that a girl would go along with it that I had a massive go at her. She tweeted me back, 'Fuck off, you fat c**t, you're not even together.' Jack even publicly taunted me about my weight or called me ugly once or twice.

Still, he'd always be full of remorse after such occasions and, like I've said before, I was definitely no angel either. My temper could be appalling. Despite how it might seem, Jack didn't behave like this often; it was quite rare, in reality. And I couldn't very well accuse him of cheating on me because we were far more 'off' than 'on'. Sometimes we had no contact for weeks on end and, of course, Matt was often at my place. It would have been massively hypocritical of me to be too unforgiving of Jack when I was spending time with this other man in my own home, wouldn't it?

In addition to all of that aggro, I can't deny that I still had affection for Matt. He was the father of my child and a part of me was desperately clinging to that.

I remember Mum saying to me, 'What's going on with you two then?'

'I honestly don't know,' I said. 'Sometimes I think that he wants to get back with me. He loves doing stuff as a family.'

'Well, that's good, isn't it?' Mum reasoned. 'Perhaps you should just make a go of it.'

'Maybe,' I said.

Around this time, I left Blakely with Mum while I went into hospital for a boob job. I wanted to get back to modelling for *Nuts* magazine and, since giving birth, my boobs had become really saggy. The op took me to a 32G cup – but having said that, my chest size fluctuates more than anyone else's I know! I have bras in every size from a D to a G and they all fit me at different times. Some days I have to wear a sports bra instead because nothing fits at all!

While I went in for the surgery, I had a cheeky bit of lipo on my arms and bum at the same time – but I didn't tell Matt about any of it because I thought he'd have a go at me.

After the op, he came over one evening and, as we were watching TV, he said, 'You look like you've lost weight.'

I guessed it was time to 'fess up. 'Ah, well, yeah. I had some lipo the other day and I had my boobs done too.'

'You look really good,' he said. 'So, can I have a look?'

'What?' I said and laughed. 'No! That's just plain weird!'

There was no way he was going anywhere near my boobs – for a start, they had ugly scars on them and he'd probably have been sick!

'Anyway,' I said. 'We're just friends, aren't we?'

He nodded. 'Couldn't we be friends and have a little kiss every now and again?'

I didn't know what to say but, swept up by the moment, we did kiss. It was so weird after all that time. But it didn't go any further and he left soon afterwards.

I was feeling more confused than ever about the future, partly because I didn't know what was going on in Matt's own love life. Then one night after Christmas, he was at mine and had just put Blakely to bed. As he was in the kitchen making us a cup of tea, his phone bleeped and I saw some girl's name next to a love-heart. I couldn't resist the urge to read back through their messages and I saw that he'd texted her earlier, 'I can't get away right now but I'll get there as soon as I can.'

She'd replied, 'Can't wait, last night was amazing.'

When I saw that, I felt sick. I'd been a total idiot. I'd obviously been reading his signals all wrong.

'Who's this girl?' I said, holding up his phone when he came back into the room.

'She's nobody. I don't like her – she's desperate.'

'It's OK, Matt. Don't feel you have to lie to me. I don't care what you do. We're not together and you're here to see Blakely, not me.'

'No, honestly. She's just a cling-on who wants to be with a footballer. We only had a drink anyway.'

I couldn't even stand to have this conversation yet again. 'OK,' I said. 'But this is all messing with my brain. Maybe you should leave now and only come round in future when Blakely is up and awake.'

'What do you mean? Why are you getting so upset?' he said, looking puzzled.

'I can't do this, Matt. We're not a couple and what you get up to is your own business.'

His body language changed completely then. He looked agitated and he jumped up to get his keys and jacket.

'Before you go, you owe me £500,' I said. 'Have you got it on you?'

'You're kidding, right?'

'No, you borrowed £500 from me, remember. I need it back.'

'Are you serious? I've bought loads of nappies and milk and you want £500 now?'

'I didn't lend you that money in exchange for nappies,' I protested. 'It wasn't my fault you didn't have your cash card. I was just helping you out.'

From out of nowhere, the malicious Matt of old reared his head again. 'Oh, here we go. I wondered how long it would be before you brought up money or your monthly maintenance.'

I felt my hackles rise. 'Great – if you've brought up the subject of maintenance, that's brilliant,' I said. 'I was waiting for you to be the one to mention it.'

He'd recently agreed to pay me a monthly income but, as a super-rich footballer, it wasn't as much as I thought he owed as Blakely's father.

'What's the big deal?' he said. 'You've got a house and you don't need a car any more.'

'The big deal, Matt, is that you are now captain of your team and I'm guessing you're earning a bloody fortune. So I think I'm entitled to more money for your son when I'm not working at the moment. Funnily enough, you can't do glamour modelling when you've got a belly the size of South Korea.'

Cagily, he said, 'I'm just going to pay for everything now, am I?'

'Well, until I've lost weight and can get a new modelling contract then, yes, I think you should cover as much as you possibly can. How will I keep my head above water if I have to dip into all my savings and start paying for things on credit cards?'

I couldn't get my head around the fact we were having this argument.

Then things got really nasty. 'You've got more equity in your house than me so, technically, you're richer than I am.'

'I'm not talking about our assets, I'm talking about our liquid capital, Matt. I haven't got many savings left because I've not worked since having the baby. I'm making a massive financial loss.'

'That's not my problem. I told you I didn't want a baby.'

Of all the hateful things Matt had ever said, this was right up there with the very worst. 'What? You've been spending all this time with your son and now you say that?'

'I didn't mean anything by it,' he backtracked. 'I was just saying that this could have been avoided.'

This was ridiculous. We were getting absolutely nowhere.

'OK, fine,' I said. 'Whatever. I don't want to argue about this. I'll just have to try and manage. All my savings will be gone soon, so we're going to have to reassess in a few months anyway.'

I was sitting on the stairs as he prepared to leave and what came out of his mouth next was like being hit head on by a bus.

'Believe me, things will get a whole lot more difficult if you ever try to get more money out of me. You'll lose everything – probably Blakely too. So just you dare trying to take me to court.'

I jumped up and slapped him around the face, really hard. 'Get out of my house right now! Get out of my life and, when you're ready to be a nice human being and see your son, call me.'

He stormed out, leaving me attempting to piece together what had just happened and how things had once again become so ugly.

CHAPTER TWENTY-SIX

See You in Court

After that argument, all contact between Matt and I ceased. Although he continued to pay me maintenance, I consulted a solicitor. I quickly discovered that it's frowned upon by the courts if you don't try to resolve financial issues through mediation first, so that's the route I agreed to take through my solicitor. Obviously, I wanted it to stay out of court – it was never about me being greedy. I just wanted to stay afloat.

To cut a very long story short, the mediation attempts throughout 2011 were a miserable failure. I don't want to sound like I was being ungrateful but I just didn't feel the proportion of his wage he was giving us was acceptable. I was a struggling single mum and I only wanted what was fair.

It was doubly difficult because I was also in the process of setting up my own cake business, called Love Cake Love Me, and was ploughing most of my own money and savings into that. It had come about after a fruitless search to find Blakely a special cake for his first birthday. The one I ordered turned out to be hopeless and I was so disappointed that I thought I could do a better job of it. So I went on several different courses about baking and decorating, set up a website, got my health-and-safety certificates and just got stuck in.

Despite so much going on in the background, Jack tried hard to be supportive and came up to see Blakely as often as he could. We also talked about the two of us moving down to Essex to be with him and got as far as booking a few house viewings. But then he bottled it at the last minute and didn't show up, so I decided the time wasn't right for such a big commitment. It was also a bad time for Jack to be making any plans like that because he'd found himself in trouble again after pleading guilty to punching a man in the head outside a nightclub in Essex. He was sentenced to a hundred hours of community service in August 2011 and the magistrate in the case told him, 'Grow up. Stop all this. Move on.' A sentiment I very much echoed – especially when I had so much serious stuff on my own plate.

While I was waiting for my case against Matt to come up at court, fate took another unexpected turn that December, when I missed a period. At first, I thought nothing of it – sometimes I had them, sometimes I didn't. My cycle was shot to pieces. My boobs had also got bigger and then my face broke out in spots – I looked like a pepperoni pizza. A few days later, my hair started looking greasy and I started feeling sick. It was time to do a pregnancy test…

Guess what? It was positive. I was like, 'For fuck's sake. How did that happen?' I knew I hadn't missed my pill but it later turned out that the antibiotics I'd recently been taking for tonsillitis must have made the pill less effective. Polycystic ovaries? Yeah, right: I seem to be a total baby-making machine.

Anyway, I wasn't sure how I felt about it. I wasn't happy or sad, although I was very worried what Jack would say and what he'd want. I was scared after what had happened with Matt and obviously fearful that might happen again.

I told Rachel first and she quickly pointed out that I was already a single mum and that Jack wasn't with me full time. 'Can you handle two children if he goes off the rails again?'

'I really don't know,' I said, truthfully.

Later that day, I told Jack. 'I don't believe you,' he said.

'Come on, why would I lie?'

Then he started grinning at me and he was so happy.

'What? You're pleased about this?'

'Well, yeah. We can have a brother or sister for Blakely. That's really nice, don't you think?'

'Er, yeah, I guess it is!' I said, smiling too.

It was such a relief that I wasn't being rejected again that I got a bit excited and told Mum and Aunty Susan while we were out shopping for Christmas cards in Marks & Spencer.

'Are you OK? You don't look well,' Mum had suddenly asked me.

'Well, I'm pregnant,' I blurted out. 'And Jack and I want to keep it.'

She and Aunty Susan were at first dumbfounded but then Mum said, 'That's fantastic!'

Despite him sometimes treating me badly, she and Dad have always liked Jack.

'Shall we buy some Babygros as we're in M&S?' she said.

'No, Mum! I don't want to buy anything yet. I need to see the doctor first. I need to get my head together.'

I went for a scan, which showed I was about four or five weeks gone. It was so much to think about. Could we even afford a baby?

Then, around 15 December, I started to get a bit of bleeding. I wasn't worried because I'd had that with Blakely too. Then I started getting occasional cramps but I'd heard that could simply be your womb stretching. On 21 December, I was still having cramps but just figured everything was OK. Then I went to the toilet and there was bright-red blood everywhere.

I went to the hospital, where a scan showed the baby hadn't changed at all in the couple of weeks between then and the first scan. It was exactly the same size, to the millimetre, and they said that, when I'd had that initial scan, I'd probably already lost it. They told me that I now had to wait for my body to expel the baby.

'How long will that take?' I asked, feeling faint.

'It could take a couple of weeks.'

'Oh, no,' I said. 'I don't want a baby inside me that's not alive.'

So they gave me the second part of an abortion tablet, which gets rid of everything quickly. Before I left, the nurse put her hand on my shoulder and said, 'The pregnancy would never have worked because the cells weren't right. Sometimes this just happens and it's not meant to be. Don't blame yourself.' It was slightly comforting to know I hadn't done anything wrong but it didn't take away the heartache.

As it was Mum's birthday and I didn't want to spoil her day, Aunty Susan came and collected me and drove me home. She got me a hot water bottle and we had a cry together. It was so very sad.

She took Blakely for a few hours to let me rest and phone Jack to break the news to him. When I did, he had literally nothing to say. He couldn't speak, other than to say, 'Oh, right. That's awful.' He's never known what to say in a crisis.

I thought he'd rush up to see me but it all went quiet. A few weeks earlier, I'd asked him to spend Christmas with Blakely and me and he had agreed, which had felt like a major breakthrough. But, in fact, he didn't come, which felt like a huge stab in the back. He just sent me a text on Christmas Day saying, 'I love you. I'm really sorry for everything.'

I was so upset that I called Mary, his mum. 'I can't believe he won't come and support me after all I've done for him,' I said. 'This is really hurtful. I had to go through my last pregnancy on my own and now Jack's done this. Why doesn't he want to do the right thing by us? He calls Blakely his son and Blakely calls him Daddy. I know he's got troubles but that doesn't excuse what he's doing to his family.'

'We're his family,' she said.

'We're his family too,' I said. 'And I do nothing but right by Jack. I stuck by him over the rape claim and did everything I could to help clear his name. He's cheated on me more times than I care to remember but I stick by him because I know it's a defence mechanism. I want to help him. I can't believe you're letting your son behave like this.'

Despite us being close before, she then said, 'Whatever. It's nothing to do with me. I'm fed up – every day there's another drama with you.'

Sobbing now, I said, 'I'm not causing the drama. I'm up here bringing up a child and trying to earn enough money to get by.'

She sighed and said, 'Look, it's you two with all the problems, so it's you two who have got to sort them out.'

'It's our problem?' I seethed. 'But when he needs financial support and picking out of the gutter, it's all of our problem, isn't it?' She hung up on me then and we've never got along too well since.

Thank God I had Blakely to get me through Christmas Day. Without him, I would have fallen apart but I had to keep going for him. You can't dwell on things or slip into despair as a parent.

On Boxing Day afternoon, Jack finally called and said, 'I'm so sorry. You know I go off the rails when I'm upset. I know I should have been there but I can't help the way I am.'

I so badly needed his support that I told him to come back up and he did. I know a lot of people say that I continually let men treat me badly but I'm a difficult person too. I argue all the time, I have a bad temper and I can be a bitch. I've not been the perfect girlfriend. I say nasty things too and Jack forgives me that. Ultimately, I can't not be there for someone I love. I believe that, if you're not there for them, you're not human.

At New Year, I got really drunk and it cheered me up, even if just temporarily. For the first time, I understood why Jack had behaved so badly after Jade died. It's a release. Sometimes you just have to drink through that pain and let it all seep out somehow.

With all the legal wrangling with Matt dragging on for what seemed like forever, the court case finally came up in spring 2012. Let's just say it didn't go well for me.

Overall, that year was just horrendous and none of my bills got paid for six months. My car was repossessed and I also had to put my house up for sale because I couldn't afford the mortgage and kept defaulting on the payments. I had 20p to my name at one point. I borrowed a bit of money from friends and family, although Mum and Dad couldn't help much – they weren't exactly flush themselves.

Some days, I was struck down with such bad depression that I couldn't get out of bed. The sadness of my miscarriage was still acute and only added to my overriding feeling of misery and worthlessness. I couldn't help thinking about how mine and Jacks' baby would have turned out, which I knew was destructive, but they were thoughts I had no control over. Mum helped me a lot with looking after Blakely, which was kind, but I felt I was trapped in this big black hole that I couldn't climb out of.

Feeling as low as ever, I turned to food for comfort. I'm an emotional eater and ploughed through anything that was in the house – crisps, chocolate, pizza, chips. You name it, I ate it. My weight soon shot up to 13st and I hated myself for that because I knew I needed to be slim to get any modelling work. It was like a vicious circle – the worse I felt, the more I ate. Then I'd feel even more miserable because I couldn't work and would just eat some more.

People have asked me if any of my previous suicidal thoughts returned when things got so bad but I can honestly say that there was never a moment when I thought about overdosing or doing something so silly again. Everything was different now because of that one little person who mattered more than anything else: Blakely. I wanted to be a part of every single day of his life and the prospect of missing out on him learning to tie his shoelaces or ride a bike would have destroyed me. I still just sit and watch him sleep sometimes – he never ceases to amaze me. You've always got something to live for when you've got a child so, even when I was destitute, I still had a purpose. Blakely was kind of like my therapy in that way, I guess.

While I'd been struggling so badly, Jack conversely appeared to have listened to that magistrate's advice and finally grown up a bit. It's true that he could still be unreliable and was in Essex for much of the time. But he did step up when I needed him. He helped massively with Blakely and would willingly change nappies, despite saying they were repulsive and the fact that they'd make him retch. And often, if we did bicker, he'd burst out laughing and say, 'Don't get cross with me, you're my wife!' He may have been joking but he would also frequently say, 'Next year I'm going to save up some money and marry you.' That was nice to hear – especially as I had started planning my wedding aged about three, when I'd wear Mum's veil and walk down the stairs pretending to marry my teddy Betsy! The best thing of all was that, if anyone asked about Jack's relationship to Blakely, he'd say, 'He is my son. I don't care who his real dad is. I'm bringing him up.'

Secure in the love of us both, Blakely was really flourishing and the first time he said, 'Mumma,' I burst into tears and called everyone in my phonebook to tell them. I then spent the next three hours trying to video him saying it again but he wouldn't do it!

Soon after that, he started saying, 'Daddy Jack,' which was so sweet. But slightly alarmingly, one of his other first words was 'ball'. He's already obsessed with football and, when he scores a goal, he pulls his T-shirt over his head and runs around, just like you see players do in matches on TV. If he ever wants to be a footballer, I won't stop him, of course, but I'll make sure he's one with morals!

The financial mess I'd landed in was an utter nightmare to try and unpick. As things spiralled out of control, I had bailiffs knocking at the door to take anything of value off me. I couldn't pay my water and electricity bills and had to sell everything – even my sofa, which was worth a couple of grand. I sold beds from my spare rooms on eBay, as well as a toaster, clothes and shoes – anything at all.

Towards the end of 2012, I was done with it. Something snapped in my head and I decided that this couldn't go on. I had to sort myself out.

From somewhere, I found a little of my old fighting spirit and came up with an action plan to get back on my feet. First up, Mum paid for me to see a private doctor, who gave me some anti-depressants. I don't like taking them but they gave me the boost I needed at such a lousy time in my life.

I also started a hardcore diet and began losing weight, which I knew would enable me to work again and start earning decent money. A few weeks later, as the pounds began dropping off, I got in touch with *Nuts* magazine, telling them, 'I'm so sorry, I've been ill this year but I'm getting back in shape again now. Do you think we could work together again?'

Fortunately for me, because I was one of their best-selling girls of all time, they agreed to give me a new contract on the proviso that I toned up a bit more. This was exactly the motivation I needed. I was never going to be a skinny little waif again but, thankfully, they seemed to like me with a few more curves than in my heyday!

After such a bleak year, *Nuts* was like my knight in shining armour. The money I got from the new contract came through just in the nick of time, as my house – which still hadn't sold, even though I'd slashed the price – was about to be repossessed. It was like someone from heaven had stepped down and said, 'Here you are. Sorted.'

In stark contrast to the year before, Christmas 2012 was full of positivity and Jack being with us throughout made both me and Blakely very happy. And as January 2013 got underway, I quickly got on with my rescue plan. I had no choice. I had a mountain of debts to clear and moping about wasn't going to get my bank manager off my case, was it?

CHAPTER TWENTY-SEVEN

A Ghost from the Past

Just as I'd vowed, I worked my arse off throughout 2013 to clear all my bills and pay back the loans I'd run up. We never went out and I was so scrimpy about everything – even down to how much hot water I'd use for Blakely's nightly bath! I never pictured myself having to watch the pennies so tightly but it was a steep learning curve that taught me a lot.

I also threw everything into making Love Cake Love Me a bigger success. And I was so pleased when it started to take off. Nowadays, it's doing so well that I'm having to turn orders down. At the moment, I'm operating out of my kitchen but, later this year, I want to open my own little shop in Horbury – and perhaps later start a franchise. The building I've got my eye on is so cute: it's like an old cottage, with gorgeous front windows and an area for a cafe and stock room, with upstairs rooms that would be perfect for the classes I've started running. It pisses me off when people send me tweets saying, 'Get a proper job.' Little do these people know that I work at least 50 hours a week and so much time and effort goes into designing, baking and decorating.

You might say that starting a cake firm was my vocation in life. Mum used to bake with me twice a week, which was always a treat, and now Blakely loves it too. We have a baking afternoon together every week and he wears a little chef's outfit, which is so adorable! Perhaps he's going to be a professional cook in later life because food is already a big passion for him. He loves singing along to One Direction videos on YouTube and, in the song 'Live While We're Young', he always changes the line 'Hey, girl, I'm waiting on you' to 'Hey, girl, I've weighed an onion'. It cracks me up.

As well as working flat out with Love Cake Love Me, I was the best-selling *Nuts* girl of 2013, so their faith in me really paid off for us both. I earned good money all year but didn't see any of it because it went on paying off every penny I owed. I could have gone under but I'm proud that I refused to. Nobody can ever tell me that I'm talentless or spoiled after I nearly lost everything. In a weird way, I'm quite pleased it all happened like that because I've definitely done it the hard way.

Matt went on to get injured again and the last I heard he was playing for Bradford City. He still has to pay me maintenance for Blakely through the CSA – but for me it's still more about the principle than the amount.

It's strange though because, no matter what I went through with Matt, I don't feel angry or bitter any more. Early last year, he had another child with a new partner and said in an interview not long afterwards, 'I've got a six-month-old baby now and you've got to think of that.' That stung badly because there was no mention of the fact that he also had a three-year-old in the form of Blakely. But again, that's his issue, not mine – and definitely not Blakely's.

Regardless of everything, I do feel strongly that I'll never stop Blakely from seeing Matt if that's the path he wants to take when he's older. They will always have an unbreakable bond by bloodline, even if they don't have any relationship. It's not up to me to dictate how that plays out. On the other hand, if Matt doesn't want anything to do with him ever again, all I can do is be there for Blakely and answer his questions honestly and sensitively. Of all people, I know exactly how hard it is to have gaping holes in your family history and I will do everything I can to shield my son from the kind of pain and trauma I went through in my younger years.

Once I'd emerged from financial ruin, things settled down between Jack and me. I finally got around to having Blakely's surname changed by deed poll, so he was now simply 'Hayes'. I didn't want my son to have this extra random name if his father had chosen to disappear from his life.

Jack clearly felt more comfortable when that was finalised – it was like the last trace of Matt had been removed from our home for good. As a result, he increased his efforts to support us both, living with us for about half the month and picking up promotional work back in Essex for the remainder. When he was away, he went out far less and was constantly on FaceTime talking to Blakely and me.

While up with us, we'd enjoy fun days out at the seaside or zoo, often with Rachel and her fiancé Jason and their toddler Sebastian – who I'm god-mum to. He and Blakely are only three months apart in age and have become inseparable. They love each other so much and always stick up for each other if any of the older kids start bossing them around in the park or the play-gym we take them to. I can see them being life-long friends – although they have been known to squabble once or twice, including over a chocolate pudding when they were both tiny. Both of them kept screaming 'Mine!' repeatedly at the other, louder and louder each time. It went on for about five minutes and Rachel and I were just falling about laughing in the background.

Despite all my efforts to entertain Blakely, I couldn't help noticing that he sometimes seemed to prefer spending time with Jack than with me! But then I guess every household has its 'Good Cop' and 'Bad Cop'. I've always set firm rules and boundaries because I want Blakely to be a grounded person, while Jack's the one who says, 'Oh, go on, just one sweet before bed then!'

I won't pretend that it wasn't good to have a man about the house too. Jack's a trained electrician, which comes in very handy, and he'd do lots of painting and decorating too. One good thing about his community service was that it had left him with loads of skills!

As spring came around, we were making plans to move in together full time and I felt like we'd turned a big corner. But then two successive interviews Jack gave in April and May 2013 inadvertently tore us apart all over again.

The first one appeared in *OK!* magazine, in which he was asked, 'Has Chanelle replaced Jade in your life?' Jack replied, 'No one could replace Jade.' In retrospect, this was a totally reasonable and innocent answer – how else could he reply? I never, ever set out to replace Jade and he knew that. It would not only have been impossible but wrong and a bit sick of me to try.

Still, I was angry at the magazine for putting Jack in that position and being disrespectful of me and my family. So in the heat of the moment, I took to Twitter (where else?) and blasted, 'As usual, a certain magazine has made me and my son dispensable. No one could replace her. Of Course. Thanks. #twistingwords.'

I couldn't leave it there though and added, 'Actually, fucking sick of living up to a ghost n never ever coming close. What's been the point in the last three years of my life then?!' For good measure, I threw in, 'Nobody will ever replace her. So living with me bringing up Blakely with me means nothing.'

Once I'd cooled down, I regretted posting the tweets and deleted them. But it made things extremely tense between Jack and me. He couldn't seem to understand my perspective and why it was so hard to hear people constantly compare me to Jade. It sounds like a bit of a cliché but sometimes it felt like there were three people in our relationship.

My tweets caused a real shit storm in the media and even my so-called friends had a go at me. In her column for *new!* magazine, Chantelle wrote:

> I was shocked when I read Chanelle Hayes' tweet about feeling like she's 'living up to a ghost' after her on-off boyfriend Jack Tweed gave an interview saying no one could replace his late wife Jade Goody.
>
> Jade's life was so tragically cut short and she left behind two little boys. How could Chanelle be so insensitive, especially now she's a mother herself?

This left me seeing red. How dare she pipe up – especially as she hadn't even got on that well with Jade? They once had a massive argument in Funky Buddha nightclub, which several people witnessed. More importantly, Chantelle was supposed to have been my friend, so I couldn't fathom why she was jumping on the bandwagon. I got that the magazine wanted her comment on it in her column but couldn't she have said something more balanced and fair?

In a fit of fury, I tweeted her, suggesting she mind her own business and concentrate on looking after her own young daughter, Dolly: 'Thanks @chantellehought for your opinion. You and Dolly should try walking in mine n Blakely's shoes before you comment.'

I also wrote, 'Coming from someone I once classed as a friend, I find the fact she's discussing me completely out of order.'

Chantelle messaged me privately on Twitter, saying something like, 'I'm really sorry – I didn't mean to upset you.'

My reply was along the lines of, 'Yes, you should be sorry. I've never slated you publicly because I care about you. I wouldn't do that to you.'

She was like, 'I know, I'm sorry but I would have been crucified if I'd taken your side. Hope you're OK. We should meet for shopping sometime.'

Once I'd calmed down, I was able to brush it all aside and accept that this is what happens when your life plays out so publicly in the media. I guess I was just upset because I thought we'd only ever say nice things about each other. But being a mum makes you realise that holding grudges is pretty silly and unimportant. We've spoken a few times since then and have remained perfectly civil but I'm sad that we'll probably never be as close as we once were. In some ways, the fact we are both young mums should mean we have more in common than ever but I guess living so far apart makes it difficult.

Anyway, Chantelle's criticism was extremely tame compared to the other vile abuse I got from complete strangers about my 'ghost' comment. Shockingly, I got death threats over it, with one psycho threatening to put a bomb on my doorstep. Another imbecile said they would pour acid on me and people shouted at me in the street things like, 'You're a second-rate Jade,' or, 'You're just Jack's sloppy seconds.' I didn't report any of it though because I didn't want to inflame the situation.

Jack and I somehow limped through that crisis but, the following month, it all kicked off again when he was offered £5,000 to be interviewed on the *Jeremy Kyle Show*.

'That's great,' I told him, knowing how much he needed the cash.

'I don't really want to do it though,' he said. 'It's got a bit of a stigma, hasn't it?'

I was surprised because it sounded like a no-brainer to me. 'Well, what's it about?'

'Oh, it's just about my partying and drinking too much. How I'm encouraging other people to live that lifestyle by being in the public eye.'

He'd surely be crazy to turn it down. 'Jack, you need the money. You should do it. How bad can that be?'

He shrugged and said reluctantly, 'I guess so.'

Half-joking, I said, 'Can I come along? I've always wanted to be in the audience at *Jeremy Kyle*.'

'No way,' he said defensively. 'You're not allowed.'

'But it's only in Manchester. I could drive you and then you wouldn't have to take the train.'

'No, you can't come,' he insisted.

I thought that was a bit odd but, when he got back from filming a few days later, he said it went fine and that Jeremy had been really nice to him. That, too, struck me as strange because, let's face it, Kyle is known for giving people a hard time, not being pally.

'Seriously?' I said. 'He's never nice to anyone. How come you got an easy ride?'

'Oh, because he asked me a few things about Jade,' he said, a bit dismissively.

The morning it aired, on 15 May, I was in the gym, when I suddenly got a load of tweets on my phone. People were saying things like, 'OMG, have you seen Jack on ITV?'

I felt sick. What was going on? I came straight home and watched the show, which I'd recorded and, of course, the whole thing was about Jade – not about his drinking or clubbing at all. I couldn't understand why he'd lied to me.

The programme, titled 'Jack Tweed: Life After Jade', focused on his heartbreak of losing her. Watching it was so upsetting, as he struggled to speak and cried throughout. He broke down as he told Jeremy how he'd left Jade's side during her final hours, which I knew had wracked him with guilt ever since.

It was hard for me to see him in so much pain and, despite trying to watch it as a neutral viewer and detach myself from it, I couldn't. There was no doubt that Jade's death was unspeakably tragic. I cried myself when I heard she'd passed away.

Then Jeremy quizzed Jack about his relationship with me, asking if we were still together. 'On and off,' said Jack, non-committedly. Jeremy mentioned that we'd both become known for our very public online bust-ups and he replied, 'She seems to live out most of our arguments on Twitter, yeah.'

Such a fleeting statement might have passed anyone else by but, for me, it was horribly wounding. That was all he could find to say about me in the entire show. There was no reference to being settled as a family with Blakely and me. Nothing. I realise he was there to talk about the loss of Jade but, after nearly three years with me, why couldn't he also be proud that he'd moved on and got some stability back in his life? I'd been the one who picked him up off the floor and built him back into some kind of decent human being.

I didn't do it for recognition or gratitude but surely being spoken about with a bit of respect wasn't too much to expect? The fact that he'd brushed me under the carpet after all I'd done for him made me feel worthless and that Blakely and I were just a cheap imitation of what he'd had before.

My disappointment led to a ferocious confrontation. 'I've had enough now!' I screamed. 'I know what you went through was awful but I want you out of my house because you have zero regard for my feelings.'

He was silent, so I carried on, saying, 'Why do you care so much about people thinking you've moved on? It doesn't mean you've stopped grieving but you should be glad you've found someone else to love you.'

Still nothing. 'I'm not having you treating Blakely like he doesn't exist,' I raged. 'You need to man up and be nice about us in public because you've been taking the fucking piss.'

Finally, he spoke, angry too. 'How selfish are you? She's died.'

'I know she has! It's awful and nobody can ever take that away. But you can't use that as an excuse for not appreciating who you're with now.'

He stormed out of the room and I phoned his mum, still in a state. But I got the cold shoulder from her. 'It's not about you,' she said. 'It was about Jade, who's dead. Have a bit of respect.'

'Are you serious?' I said. 'I know full well it's not about me. But all he needed to do was say, "Yeah, we're happy, things are going well." I didn't want to be called the greatest person that ever existed, I just wanted him to acknowledge that he, Blakely and I are a family unit.'

Maybe I was overreacting, I don't know, but I stuck to my guns and made Jack move out, confirming our split on Twitter:

> Just to clarify re Jeremy Kyle interview today. I think Jack did very well and admire him for his commitment to jade in the later part of her life. It is overwhelmingly clear to me we shouldn't have ever entered a relationship when he was still so badly grieving this fact was never made clear to me and was always denied by him regardless of the support I offered to him.
>
> Lately, the toll of this has caused us to come to the decision that him staying with us when he is not yet ready to move on from the love of his life is simply unfair to all involved. I wish Jack all the best for the future and hope that he manages to learn to deal with his grief and be happy finally.

It was a thoroughly miserable time and Blakely cried continually for Jack – who I knew missed him just as badly. I felt like the wicked witch for keeping them apart.

Two weeks after the show, I was still adamant I didn't want Jack back, but he called me and said, 'Look, I know I should have said something nice about you but I was put on the spot. I'm truly sorry.'

'That's not good enough, I'm afraid.'

But he was desperate. 'This is stupid. I've not been eating or sleeping. There's no way I want this family torn apart by a stupid interview on TV. It's ridiculous. We've been through far worse than this. You seriously need to get over it now.'

Something about his words struck a chord with me: perhaps I did need to get over it. In the cold light of day, the facts were simple: I loved Jack and I knew he loved me too. Without him, I felt like I had a limb missing and I knew he was undoubtedly the most important man in my life to date. What's more, as a parenting unit, we were doing a brilliant job of bringing up our son and that was a big factor to take into account.

So, yes, Jack moved back in with us in summer 2013. Once again, people may accuse me of being crazy to get back with him but what else can you trust other than your gut instinct? In spite of everything, I still see the good in him and it far outweighs any bad or the times he's been a bastard to me. You could probably count the terrible things he's done to me on two hands but, in the four years he's been part of my life, there have literally been thousands of nice gestures and moments to cherish – such as the holiday to Tunisia I booked for the three of us straight after he moved back.

Blakely hadn't been away since he was 10 months old and he loved the whole experience of getting on a plane and being somewhere hot and sunny. His delight and enthusiasm for everything made Jack and me as excitable as little kids as well and the whole holiday was brilliant. The hotel was stunning and Blakely adored splashing about in the pool for hours on end. The three of us also went on camel rides and excursions into the desert, where we dressed up in traditional Tunisian clothes. And every night, we ate an early dinner overlooking the beach, before taking Blakely to the disco, where he showed off all his slick moves to the little girls! Even now, almost a year on, he asks me continually, 'Mummy, when can we live in a hotel again?' He gets this look of concentration on his face and says, 'It's freezing here every day. It hasn't been sunny for years, has it?' Seriously, he talks like an old pensioner sometimes! The trip was exactly what Jack and I needed too; proper, quality time together as a family without any phones or stress.

Since then, our home life has been much calmer and, eight months on, we're making a real go of it. He's proved himself to be a good dad and a good partner and we've both realised we function better when we're together than when we're apart.

Jack loves treating me and coming up with little surprises and, on my birthday in November, he got up with Blakely at 5am to bake me a cake, which they topped with my absolute favourite chocolate bar – Kinder Bueno! In all honesty, it looked a bit like tuna fish but it tasted gorgeous! They also hung 'Happy Birthday' banners and streamers everywhere and blew up a load of helium balloons, before giving me tons of presents and the best breakfast in bed. Blakely now keeps asking me when my next birthday is so they can do it again!

I've also had a constantly bad knee for the past six months and Jack has bent over backwards to help me do the things I've struggled with. He even learned to vacuum so that I didn't have to do it – although, between you and me, he's no Mrs Doubtfire and I always secretly redo it!

For the first time, he's also tried hard to immerse himself in life up north and has worked at getting to know my friends better. He and Zoe's other half, Martin, often disappear to the pub for whole weekends at a time to watch football, rugby, cricket, or any kind of sport. They'd probably sit through the World Chess Championship if it meant they could drink a few pints in peace! Zoe and I love it though because, while they're off doing their male-bonding bit, we open a bottle of Châteauneuf-du-Pape (the current favourite) and get stuck into a French-cheese platter while putting the world to rights.

Feeling brighter about his own prospects, Jack's now starting a new business venture, which will help enable him to provide for Blakely and me in the future. And with my career going steadily too, the next few years are full of all kinds of possibility. Of course, we still argue and we probably always will – although never in earshot of Blakely, I hasten to add. But show me a couple who doesn't fight? They don't exist.

While a lot of men would simply have found a single mum with a toddler an inconvenience, Jack has only ever showered Blakely with love, affection and endless amounts of fun. And whatever your personal view of us as a couple, my son is at his very happiest when he's with his mummy and his daddy, and the sound of our laughter fills the house.

It really is as simple as that.

Epilogue

W hat can I say about the experience of telling you my story? It's certainly been a challenge to confront some of these memories and get them down on paper.

What I have realised in reading it all back is that, in my 26 years so far, I've probably experienced more sad things than the average person will endure in a lifetime. But there's no way I want to sit and wallow in it or say 'poor me'. I refuse to play the victim card – I firmly believe you're only a victim if you let yourself be.

Now I've got my share of hardship out of the way, I'm kind of hoping my next 26 years (and all of those thereafter) are filled with a bigger slice of the good stuff. I can't wait to see what Blakely grows up to be and I hope I'm lucky enough to have more children in a few years and be happily married too.

So many wonderful things have come out of the bad for me and this was perfectly illustrated at Blakely's third birthday party last summer. I'd thrown a circus-themed party in my back garden with a bouncy castle and all the kids' faces were painted.

Everyone was really happy that day and, as I looked around me and saw all the people I loved, it was like the cast list of my life: Jack, Blakely, Mum, Dad and David were there, alongside my Aunty Susan and Uncle Paul, my sister Melissa, her lovely partner Dillian and their four-year-old twin girls, Africa and Aamori. Then there were all my closest friends too – Rachel and her fiancé Jason with little Seb, as well as Zoe and Martin, Alison and Becca.

It brought home to me the fact that, no matter how broken and messed up things had been in the past for me, my friends and my whole family – both blood and adoptive – had pulled together to get me through it.

And as Blakely begged his cousins Africa and Aamori to play football with him and they instead covered him with make-up and put sparkly clips in his hair, I was filled with a gratitude that almost took my breath away. It was one of those split-second moments that proves, whatever else might be going on behind the scenes, by far the most important thing in life are the people in it. Wealth and success pale into insignificance in the grand scheme of it all.

How best to summarise my tale? Well, I've had tough days and, yes, at certain times I've felt like I couldn't go on but I proved to myself that I could. And I did. It's not like I'm sitting on millions of pounds and have conquered the world but I've beaten a hell of a lot of demons and that's enough for me.

To everyone who helped me along the way, thank you. I'm certain you all know who you are...